Media Audiences

Media Topics

Series editor: Valerie Alia

Titles in the series include:

Media Audiences
Television, Meaning and Emotion

Kristyn Gorton

Edinburgh University Press

© Kristyn Gorton, 2009

Edinburgh University Press Ltd
22 George Square, Edinburgh

Typeset in Janson and Neue Helvetica
by Servis Filmsetting Ltd, Stockport, Cheshire and
printed and bound in Great Britain by
CPI Antony Rowe, Chippenham and Eastbourne

A CIP record for this book is available from the British Library

ISBN 978 0 7486 2417 1 (hardback)
ISBN 978 0 7486 2418 8 (paperback)

The right of Kristyn Gorton
to be identified as author of this work
has been asserted in accordance with
the Copyright, Designs and Patents Act 1988.

Contents

Acknowledgements

As with all books, there are many people to thank for getting to this point. I am grateful to my colleagues in the Department of Theatre, Film & Television, University of York, for their generous support: Andrew Tudor, Mike Cordner, Mary Luckhurst, Sandra Pauletto, Andrea Potts, John Mateer and Paul Ryan. Many thanks as well to my MA/PhD students for letting me rehearse some of these ideas on them: Martin Zeller, Claire Swarbrick, Noelani Peace, Chris Hogg, Hsaio-Chen Chang, Ramida Vijitphan, Junna Wang and John Saddington, and to Gabrielle Griffin and Corinna Tomrley in the Women's Studies Centre. Thanks to colleagues outside York: Sara Ahmed, Jackie Stacey, Lance Pettitt, Dave Webb, Steve Wright, Julia Hallam, Vicki Ball, Amy Holdsworth, Joanne Garde-Hansen, Ros Jennings, Sherryl Wilson, Abigail Gardner, Josie Dolan and to Philip Rayner (for early help in understanding the audience). I owe a great debt to Paul Blackledge, Lisa Taylor and Alison Peirse for reading drafts.

Special thanks to participants from the television industry whose contribution has been invaluable: Kay Mellor, Belinda Johns, Brigie de Courcy, Kevin McGee, Anita Turner, Lisa Holdsworth and Steve Frost. Many thanks to family and friends for their insights and encouragement: Margie and John Wheeler, David and Cathy Watterson, Meggan and Andrew Watterson, Elizabeth Wheeler, Tracy and Kirk Ritari, Joanne Blackledge, Jane and Maier Driver, Catherine Porter, Esther Wohlgemut, Louisa Tamplin, Jamie Murphy, Trevor and Gill Griffiths and Colin and Ewa Barker. Special thanks to Liz for helping with the cover.

Many thanks to Valerie Alia, Esmé Watson and Sarah Edwards at Edinburgh University Press for their generous support, patience and editorial advice.

This book is dedicated to Patricia O'Neill, for inspiring me to teach and for debates on television and nineteenth-century poetry; and to my stepsons: Johnny and Matthew, who faithfully, and with much emotion, watch *The Simpsons*, believing it is what I teach. Finally, and as ever, I want to thank Paul Blackledge for being the kind of person he is and for nights with *The Sopranos*.

Versions of Chapters 4, 6, 7 and the 'Learning to love the Mafia' section of Chapter 8 have appeared in the following journals: *Feminist Theory, Journal of British Cinema and Television, Critical Studies in Television* and *Feminism & Psychology*; a version of Chapter 9 appeared in S. Gillis and J. Hollows (eds), *Feminism, Domesticity and Popular Culture* (Routledge, 2008).

Preface: emotion, engagements and orientation

My interest in television, meaning and emotion began when I was thinking about how emotion could be understood as an aesthetic quality that made for good television (Gorton 2006). Initially this question led me to research within anthropology of the media – in particular to S. Elizabeth Bird's *The Audience in Everyday Life: Living in a Media World* (2003). Bird's work was influential for many reasons: her conceptualisation of the audience as active *and* passive enables us to think more practically about the ways people encounter television in their everyday lives; she remind us that 'The images and messages wash over us, but most leave little trace, unless they resonate, even for a moment, with something in our personal or cultural experience' (2003: 2). Most of our television watching experience is spent unmarked. However, as Bird points out, there are moments which resonate either with personal or cultural experiences, and which therefore stand out and are imprinted in our memories. One person I interviewed, for instance, vividly remembers the episode of *Neighbours* when Madge, a long-term character, dies. She describes watching a programme of 'important moments in television' and having to turn away from the screen when this moment was aired. She explains, 'I can't look because it brings back that moment when it actually happened, and I'm like "Oh, Madge is dying all over again, and I don't want to see it"' (Interview 13/2/8). These moments are familiar to many of us and signal an emotional engagement with television. This book is interested in these moments – how they tell us something about television aesthetics, the audience and the concept of emotion.

This book is also interested in the 'turning away' described by the viewer; she had to literally look away from the screen to avoid the emotional moment she experienced years ago. Around the same time I first read Bird's book I attended a talk given by Professor Sara Ahmed. Following her influential work on the concept of emotion in *The Cultural Politics of Emotion* (2004), Ahmed considered the notion of 'orientation' in relation to sexuality, later developed into *Queer*

Phenomenology: Orientations, Objects, Others (2006). Focusing on the concept of orientation as understood within phenomenology, Ahmed argues that: 'To be orientated is also to be turned toward certain objects, those that help us to find our way ... They might be landmarks or other familiar signs that give us our anchoring points' (2006: 1). Although Ahmed is thinking about orientation and objects in terms of queer sexuality, her notion of orientation reminded me of the ways in which we orientate ourselves in front of the television. Whether we turn off the lights, gather up a blanket and hold a glass of wine or whether we pull out a table and put some food on it in preparation for our viewing experience – there seems to be a way in which people use the television as an 'anchoring point' and as something to orient their everyday lives around. If we return to the idea of particular 'moments' which draw us in, then I think we must add the way in which we orientate ourselves towards these moments. In other words, I think the way we orient ourselves towards what we watch and these moments that resonate with personal and cultural experience are intimately linked. I am grateful to both Bird's and Ahmed's work for providing the inspiration for this book and hope it continues an interest in emotion, orientation and engagement in others.

To Patricia O'Neill, an inspirational teacher and to Johnny and Matthew, who didn't shed a tear while watching *Bambi*

Introduction: why study television?

The question of why television should be studied needs to be addressed first since it is often an implicit one that students, academics and interested readers ask themselves when they pick up a book on television. Those more sceptical might even ask: can you study television? Television studies has been an academic discipline since the 1970s and comes from a variety of disciplines including literary theory, social sciences, journalism and linguistic theory. It is studied in universities and is either taught in departments that also teach theatre and film or exists as a primary component in departments that focus on the media, cultural studies and/or mass communication. Television studies is firmly rooted within the humanities and social sciences and has an advantage in that it can draw from a wide range of theoretical approaches and methodologies. It focuses primarily on issues involving representation, genre, the industry, textual analysis and audience reception. In his introduction to *Television Studies* Toby Miller points out that '[t]he intellectual genealogy of television studies is formidable and very interdisciplinary' (2002: 1).

Even though television studies is accepted as an academic discipline it is often one that is misunderstood and even misrepresented by others. There is a continual suggestion of TV's 'dumbing down', which is often true of the cheap programming available en masse, but which unfairly dismisses the significant developments and achievements of television programming in what has been referred to as TV3 (Nelson 2007; see also *New Review of Film and Television*, 5(1), 2007). Indeed, one of the central arguments in Robin Nelson's excellent study of 'high-end' television is that TV dramas in TV3 are as good if not better than TV dramas in the past which contradicts discourses on the 'dumbing down' of television (2007: 161). Television continues to be the most accessible mode of communication in the world and is therefore an incredibly important medium to understand and study.

However, it is not enough just to watch television: a viewer needs to be aware of the kind of watching they are doing and this has to do with engagement. Are you idly watching or paying attention? Most of us will know the difference and therefore understand that simply watching television is not the same as studying it. We have some sense from our own viewing patterns that there are times when we are very engaged with what we watch and others when we are simply sitting in front of the screen to pass time. The difference between these moments is often marked by our emotional response to what we are watching – hence I shall argue that emotion is an important territory to be considered within a study of television audiences.

But how do we study television? Nelson suggests that it is important to

> undertake both textual analysis to bring out the qualities of television programmes and to engage in what John Corner calls "expanded criticism". That is to say, the contingency of critical readings must be acknowledged through self-reflection and both texts and judgements of them should be located in the force-field of influences upon them. (2007: 163)

Nelson suggests that these central influences include: economic, political, institutional, aesthetic and technological developments (2007: 163). Part of the study of television, as Nelson argues, is locating your research within a broader theoretical framework. In a special edition of *Cinema Journal* questioning the 'place' of television studies today (2005), Horace Newcomb argues that we must 'ask questions that help explain to others why television continues to be so important' (2005: 111). Newcomb's point is an increasingly important one as it is necessary for television studies to continue a tradition of both seeing what the medium does and what is done to it; of addressing the 'larger social and cultural constructs that surround us' (2005: 111). Extending beyond Newcomb's point, I think it is also important to recognise that we have reached a point within television studies where we should also be concerned with more specific issues, such as emotion and aesthetics.

Guilty pleasures

Given that this book focuses on emotion – I want to begin by drawing out the emotion of guilt. This emotion is most often associated with television watching. If someone asked you what you did last night and all you did was sit on the couch and watch television, you are very likely to reply 'nothing'. People feel guilty and are made to feel guilty for watching too much television because it is seen as lazy and unproductive. Many will remember being warned as a child not to sit too close to the television or to go outside and play instead of staying in to watch television. While not in favour of a culture that sits around watching television all day, I am instead pointing out the way we are acculturated to feel guilt in association with television watching. For this guilt leads to a devaluation of the television watching experience. As Raymond Williams suggests:

> [M]ost of us say, in describing the experience, that we have been "watching television," rather than that we have watched "the news" or "a play" or "the football on television". Certainly we sometimes say both, but the fact that we say the former at all is already signifi-cant. ([1974] 1992: 94)

Instead of valuing the particular television programme watched, viewers often describe the experience in more general terms: 'watching telly' is often then synonymous with doing nothing or just passing time.

One of the notable findings in David Gauntlett and Annette Hill's excellent study of 'television, culture and everyday life' points to the guilt people feel when watching television. Respondents to their Audience Tracking Study were asked, 'Do you ever feel guilty about watching television?' This question revealed a high proportion of people who felt guilty for 'wasting time' in connection with television viewing. The guilt ranged from feelings about wasting time (in lieu of doing something more constructive) to feelings of guilt about 'trashy tastes' (1999: 119–28). However, despite these feelings, most respond-ents did not seem motivated to do something about this guilt – either, as Gauntlett and Hill suggest, because the television programmes were so compelling or because they were not *that* guilty about it in the first place. The latter analysis suggest that people often feel guilty about television watching because they have been encouraged to associate television watching with laziness and passivity. And yet at the same time, television programmes are continually lauded as significant examples of social critique. *The Wire*, for instance, has received unprecedented attention for its portrayal of urban poverty in America. In a panel at Harvard University, Professor William Julius Wilson argued that: '[*The Wire*] has done more to enhance an understanding of the challenges of urban life and the problems of urban inequality than any other media event or scholarly publication, including studies by social scientists' (http://www.iop.harvard.edu/Multimedia-Center/All-Videos/The+HBO-Series-TheWire-A-Compelling-Portrayal-of-an-American-City). Similarly, *Battlestar Galactica* has been hailed as offering 'the most serious, sustained and never cut-and-dry look on television at life in a post-9/11 world' by academics, fans and viewers.[1]

Indeed a conference was held in the UK regarding its political and social explanatory power. In both examples, television programmes are deemed capable of orientating people's political ideas, their emotions and their approach to the world.

New viewing practices

The debate over whether television audiences are passive or active has characterised media research for four decades, since the founding of television studies as an academic discipline. Although there are historical and social reasons why some generations of researchers have imagined the audience as active and others have perceived them as passive, arguments that will be explored in more detail in Chapter 1, it is perhaps most useful to think of the audience as active, but at times passive, and never completely knowable. As S. Elizabeth Bird argues: 'the "audience" is everywhere and nowhere' (2003: 3).

On average, most students I have asked admit that they have at least four television sets per home. Usually this means that there is a television set in the main family room, the kitchen and in each bedroom. The lower cost and availability of television sets and the variance in size means that a television can be anywhere in our home and implies new viewing practices. For many, watching television is no longer a family affair, although many people will get together over one programme in particular. Almost all my students have television watching 'groups' who watch ritually with each other and, if apart, communicate by text about the programme. There remains a way in which television is often shared and is seen as a communal experience. Chat rooms that exist for almost every television programme attest to the ways in which people connect over their favourite show. But what does it mean to bond over a television programme? What is shared? The characters, the plot, the narrative? What draws us in so intensely and what are we emotionally attached to? This book will focus in particular on the ways in which television programmes affect their viewers.

We must also consider how new technologies, such as DVR recording devices (TiVo for instance) and an increase in sales and availability of DVD box sets create new ways of viewing television. Handheld television devices also mean that television features more prominently in our lives than ever before. Indeed, we can argue that there are more irrational patterns in viewing where people watch television on their handheld recording devices than when they sit in front of the television in their homes (Morley 2006). Increasing convergence within media texts – between internet, television and film – has meant that we must think about how we watch differently. Indeed, Virginia Nightingale argues that television is becoming more like the internet and the internet is becoming more like television (2007). Nelson points out that some people are already reading their emails through their television and argues that 'increasingly the ubiquitous domestic small screens, through sharing digital technology, will become one' (2007: 12). The move towards digitalisation, for instance, will also greatly impact what we watch and how we watch it and will, as some argue, radically alter our relationship to television. But do these new viewing practices, which are more personalised and anchored around lifestyle, 'mean that television is *less* central or *more* central to our ways of life'? Helen Wood and Lisa Taylor pose this interesting question in their work on television audiences and argue that we may never find the answers 'if prevailing discourses of new media force us to ask entirely different questions' (2008: 146). In other words, if we lose sight of the intimate relationship viewers have with television in favour of seeing television as simply part of media convergence, then we will also overlook important questions and research that aims to interrogate the specificities of television and its audience.

Finally, it is necessary to make distinctions about television watching practices versus cinematic viewing experiences: and here we can think about the difference between the cinematic 'gaze' (Metz 1975; Mulvey 1975); the televisual 'glance' (Ellis 1983, cited in Moore 1989: 50) and what a theorist has referred to as the 'glaze' (Goldblatt).[2] Watching television is not the same experience as viewing a film. The differences in these ways of seeing and their relationship to television and film will be discussed in more detail in Chapters 2 and 5.

Get into it

The phrase, 'get into it', is one I have heard used by students and colleagues alike when describing a new television series, such as *24*, *Lost*, *Heroes* and *The Wire*. It refers to the experience of getting involved with a new programme and means that it might take the viewer a few episodes before she 'gets into it'. This book is particularly interested in the ways viewers 'get into' what they watch – how they become emotionally engaged with programmes. It is also interested in thinking through emotion as an aesthetic quality that makes for good television. Part of what the phrase 'get into it' implies is that it is worth 'getting into'. It suggests that, although the viewer might not be hooked at first, the programme will eventually draw its viewer in and make it worth the effort of staying with the programme. The fact that this phrase is often used with regard to popular shows such as *The Sopranos* (HBO 1999–2007) is further evidence that the success of a television programme and its reception depends in part on the emotional investment the viewer makes.

Drawing on research on emotion and affect from feminist theory and film theory, this book will focus on emotion in television. In the first half of the book, I shall offer some theoretical background on emotion and affect. The second half will focus more specifically on case studies – on ways in which we can think about emotion and affect in terms of television studies. The case studies will offer textual readings of emotion, they will consider the more technical aspects of how emotion is constructed, and the final chapter will consider how we can research the use of emotion in ethnographic projects.

This book seeks to do many things but is primarily designed to offer an introduction to the study of the audience within television studies; to focus in particular on feminist research on television; and, finally, to argue that recent work on emotion and affect allows us to think about television and its meaning to the audience in new ways.

Notes

1. Lynne Joyrich, Associate Professor of Modern Culture and Media, Brown University, argues: 'Though an entertainment program, *Battlestar Galactica* offers the most serious, sustained and never cut-and-dry look on television at life in a post-9/11 world.' She goes on to explain that: 'While the show's premise may seem simple . . . it engages viewers to review their own stories, histories and possible futures by blurring the lines between literal and figurative messages' (cited in Roehrkasse 2007: 1).
2. David Goldblatt argues that television has also produced the 'glaze', 'where a stupid, glassy stare has replaced a more attentive or alert viewing' (2002: 74), and argues that remote controls and channel-surfing are partly to blame. Goldblatt's configuration of the 'glaze' is important in the sense that it would be silly to discount the times when people do just stare into the screen without much engagement.

Exercises

Examine the content pages of television studies texts (such as those listed below in 'Further reading'). What are these collections primarily concerned with? (Note: this idea comes from Brunsdon 1998.)

Questions for discussion

1. Do you agree that guilt is often associated with television watching? Discuss the cultural reasons for your answer.
2. What does the phrase 'get into it' mean to you? Have you ever been a fan of a particular programme? Is there a difference between someone who is an avid watcher of a programme and a fan? Discuss these differences.
3. How do you imagine emotion can be discussed in terms of television?

Further reading

Allen, Robert C. and Annette Hill (eds) (2004), *The Television Studies Reader*, London and New York: Routledge.

Burton, Graeme (2000), *Talking Television: An Introduction to the Study of Television*, London: Arnold.

Bignell, Jonathan (2004), *An Introduction to Television Studies*, London: Routledge.

Brunsdon, Charlotte (1998), 'What is the television of Television Studies?', in Christine Geraghty and David Lusted (eds), *The Television Studies Book*, London: Hodder Arnold, pp. 95–113.

Corner, John (1999), *Critical Ideas in Television Studies*, Oxford: Clarendon Press.

Crisell, Andrew (2006), *A Study of Modern Television: Thinking inside the Box*, Basingstoke: Palgrave Macmillan.

Fiske, John (1992), *Television Culture*, London: Routledge.

Geraghty, Christine and David Lusted (eds) (1998), *The Television Studies Book*, London: Arnold.

Hilmes, Michelle (2003), *The Television History Book*, London: British Film Institute.

Miller, Toby (2002), *Television Studies*, London: British Film Institute.

Newcomb, Horace (ed.) (2000), *Television: The Critical View*, Oxford: Oxford University Press.

Wood, Helen and Lisa Taylor (2008), 'Feeling sentimental about television audiences', *Cinema Journal*, 47(3): 144–51.

Part One

Theoretical background

1 'Desperately Seeking the Audience': models of audience reception

Audiences are problematic. (Abercrombie and Longhurst 1998: 1)

The Who's 'Who are you?' is the theme song for one of the most popular and widely viewed television programmes in the US and the UK: *CSI*. It functions as a provocative opening and a pun as one of the central themes of the programme is to find out 'whodunit'. It also serves as a useful juxtaposition – the earthy, rock tones of The Who bellow out in contrast to the high-tech sophistication offered by the forensic investigating team. This question, 'who are you?', is also at the forefront of audience studies. Who are *you* the viewing public and what do *you* want to watch. This question has perplexed researchers, producers, writers and executives since the inception of television.

In the preface to her influential study of audiences, Ien Ang tells us 'that despite television's apparently steady success in absorbing people's attention, television audiences remain extremely difficult to define, attract and keep. The institutions must forever "desperately seek the audience"' (1991: ix). One of the central arguments in this book is that emotion is central to this seeking of the audience. Writers and producers understand the importance of moving their audiences and audiences value television programmes on the basis of their ability to move them. Ang's work aimed to disrupt a notion of the audience as unified and controllable and to reintroduce a sense of irony about this mass of people watching television (1991: ix–x). Another part of her project is to consider how industry professionals account for 'popular television in the realm of everyday life' (1991: x); in other words, what does the industry make of audience's everyday engagement with television? The emphasis in this book is both on audiences and their emotional engagement. Like Ang, I want to deconstruct the notion of audiences as fixed and controllable and want to focus on the ways in which television is part of most people's everyday landscape.

How can we understand the audience? What exactly does this term refer to and how can we begin to map out the history of research on the audience? This chapter does not intend to be fully comprehensive, rather it will critically outline some of the ways in which the audience has been approached, theorised and researched. I shall also suggest that the term audience is one that needs to be re-defined and reconsidered in light of new and developing television watching practices.

The history of audience research is characterised by a division between powerful media and powerful viewers: that is, between understanding the media as capable of influencing and therefore affecting viewers and understanding viewers as capable of influencing and therefore affecting the media.

The audience

How can we define 'the *audience*'? Is an audience more than one person, a group of people, a crowd, a mob or a small gathering? Are they simply watching or is there a level of engagement we should expect from them? What are the differences we can think of between a theatre audience, a film audience and a television audience? In asking these questions we can begin to appreciate how daunting the word 'audience' can be and how many different ways we can think about the term with regards to the media. As Ross and Nightingale suggest: '[t]he word *audience* is so much part of our everyday talk that its complexity is often taken for granted' (2003: 4, authors' italics). However, if we think about the differences between a theatre, film and television audience we may consider the following categories as points of distinction and definition:

- Level of activity
- Space
- Time constraints
- Accessibility
- Interaction
- Proximity
- Concentration

For instance, it is likely that you will know the exact times for a film or a theatre performance and the place in which you will watch the performance, but you might not be as exact about the times of a television programme or in which room you will watch the programme you have in mind. Sitting in a theatre is inevitably different and more constrained than sitting on the couch with a blanket wrapped around you. Television continues to be the most accessible media, and although viewers pay a licence fee in the UK to watch it, it is cheaper and more available than a theatre performance or film. Our concentration may vary but it is more likely that you will feel forced to 'pay attention' to a theatre performance; whereas you are allowed to doze off or just leave a television programme. If we think of something as simple as dress – you can imagine that you would make an effort to wear something presentable to a play, while you can be watching television naked in the comfort of your own home. These are relatively simple and straight-forward distinctions we can readily draw between the different kinds of audiences for theatre, film and television but they point toward the difficulty in knowing an audience and their needs.

If we consider television audiences more specifically we can also start to consider how the audience is presented on screen. Think about the different presentations of audiences in the talk show genre, for instance. Here we have a variety of ways in which the audience is used to tell us something about the presenter's style and engagement. Donahue and Kilroy (talk show hosts) walked around their audiences soliciting answers to the questions the guests posed. They walked among their guests as if part of them, and one of them, thus creating little distinction between them as 'expert' and their audience as 'witnesses'. In contrast, *Oprah* and *Dr Phil* (talk shows) often used a raised platform where they would sit with their guests. Their audiences were there to watch and feel close to them, but not part of them.

It is also important to distinguish between *audience* as a concept and the actual audiences that we inhabit whether in a theatre, cinema, or living room. Ang draws a theoretical distinction between '"television audience" as discursive construct and the social world of actual audiences' (1991: 13). These two things might not always be the same and we must be aware of the differences between them. The term 'audience' itself might no longer adequately describe the groups of people watching television – but for the time being it is the concept we have available and yet one loaded with historical, cultural and political implications.

A brief history of audience research

This section provides a brief sketch of the debates regarding models of the audience since the 1930s. It is intended to set the stage for more recent developments in audience reception and to provide a background to later discussions on emotion and audiences. It is necessary to understand how the audience has been perceived in critical and cultural theory before considering more specific issues regarding emotion and meaning. However, this is only a brief background and the reading at the end of this chapter should encourage more detailed research of the developments outlined.

One starting place might be with the Frankfurt School (Institute of Social Research), particularly Adorno and Horkheimer's work on the cultural industries. The rise of Nazi occupation in Germany and fascism in Italy demonstrated the power of mass propaganda and the ability of music and other popular forms to ideologically control its audiences. In the introduction to *The Dialectic of Enlightenment*, Adorno and Horkheimer assert that '[t]here is no longer any available form of linguistic expression which has not tended toward accommodation to dominant currents of thought' (1979: xii) and argue later, in their chapter on 'the culture industry' that '[f]ilms, radio and magazines make up a system which is uniform as a whole and in every part' (1979: 120). Adorno and Horkheimer's move to Los Angeles in the 1940s to escape Nazi occupation had a direct influence on their theoretical ideas. The star industry, very different to the celebrity culture of today (see Gamson 1994; Rojek 2001), epitomised the way Hollywood manufactured and produced its stars and movies in a kind of factory conveyor belt style. Adorno and Horkheimer argue that the industry created 'dupes' of the masses – that they would mindlessly consume the latest version of the same thing without question. They write: 'No independent thinking must be expected from the audience: the product prescribes every reaction: not by its natural structure (which collapses under reflection), but by signals. Any logical connection calling for mental effort is painstakingly avoided' (1979: 137). Importantly for this work, Adorno and Horkheimer's evaluation of the culture industry lead them to conclude that

> The most intimate reactions of human beings have been so thoroughly reified that the idea of anything specific to themselves now persists only as an utterly abstract notion: personality scarcely signifies anything more than shining white teeth and freedom from body odour and emotions. The triumph of advertising in the culture industry is that consumers feel compelled to buy and use its products even though they see through them. (1979: 167)

Here they suggest that, even when aware of being manipulated, consumers will take pleasure and buy the products of the culture industry without question. So they are suggesting not simply that consumers are dupes, unaware of the constructed nature of the products they enjoy, but that, even in their awareness, they buy them anyway. In *Media, Gender and Identity*, for instance, David Gauntlett explains this dynamic as follows:

> The teen 'rebels' who are fans of [Eminem or Marilyn Manson], Adorno would suggest, are just consumers: buying a CD is not

rebellion, it's buying a CD. The tough guy who has just bought the latest angry rap CD, takes it home and plays it loud, may be thinking, 'Yeah! Fuck you, consumer society!', but as far as Adorno is concerned, he might as well say, 'Thank you, consumer society, for giving me a new product to buy. This is a good product. I would like to make further purchases of similar products in the near future. (2002: 21)

Adorno's work exemplifies the notion of the media as a powerful agent of control and the audience as a passive receiver. His work was later to be questioned by writers such as John Fiske whose *Understanding Popular Culture* (1989a) and *Reading the Popular* (1989b) suggest that individuals give mass-cultural art forms personal meaning, and in so doing actively engage with them. He argues in *Understanding Popular Culture* that:

> Popular culture is made by the people, not produced by the culture industry. All the culture industries can do is produce a repertoire of texts or cultural resources for the various formations of the people to use or reject in the on-going process of producing their popular culture. (1989a: 24)

For instance, where Adorno might see Madonna as an example of someone who manufactures music to be consumed for profit, Fiske argues that her music captures the spirit of generations of women. He writes: 'Her image becomes, then, not a model of meaning for young girls in patriarchy, but a site of semiotic struggle between the forces of patriarchal control and feminine resistance, of capitalism and the subordinate, of the adult and the young' (Fiske 1989b: 97).

This sets up a debate between the consumer as 'passive dupe' or as 'active agent' – a debate that characterises work on audiences and is one we can continue to argue today. Lawrence Grossberg's work, for example, illustrates a continuing interest in configuring the audience as active and in troubling the concept of audience altogether. He argues that:

> Audiences are constantly making their own cultural environment from the cultural resources that are available to them. Thus, audiences are not made up of cultural dupes; people are often quite aware of their own implication in structures of power and domination, and of the ways in which cultural messages (can) manipulate them. Furthermore, the audience of popular culture cannot be conceived of as a singular homogeneous entity; we have to take seriously the differences within and between the different fractions of the popular audience. (1992a: 53)

As Grossberg suggests, not only are audiences aware of the ways in which they are manipulated by the media but also, we, as scholars, need to be careful to resist simplifying the notion of audience and instead appreciate the differences that exist in different sub-groups and demographics.

In the 1950s, Katz and Lazarsfeld (1955) advanced the 'two-step' flow model of communication, which suggested that 'ideas often flow from radio and print to opinion leaders and from these to the less active sections of the population' (1957: 61). This model challenged the notion of the mass media as dominant over the audience and emphasised the role interpersonal relations play in communication. Their model illustrates a more negotiated understanding of the relationship between powerful media and powerful audiences. However, this work was followed in the 1960s by experimental behaviourist research that reiterated the idea of powerful media and considered the way in which innocent children could be helplessly moulded into social roles. Bandura and Walters's *Social Learning and Personality Development* (1963) is one of the first pieces of research to consider what we now refer to as the 'media effects' debate. Their experiments suggested that children who watch violent events on screen will perform similar actions on other children, or, in the case of their research, on a 'bobo' doll. Although their work has been criticised by many theorists,[1] the question of whether violence on screen affects children continues to perplex researchers and is a topic often taken up by journalists. Indeed, the case of James Bulger and the assumption generated by the media that *Child's Play 3* affected the boys who killed Bulger is still part of British cultural imagination. The death of James Bulger prompted a 'moral panic' (see Cohen [1972] 2002) that still resonates today. The issue of children and television (for instance, see Lemish 2007) continues to be a strong, developing part of audience research as is the idea of 'media effects' – perhaps best explored in a collection entitled *Ill Effects: The Media/Violence Debate* (Barker and Petley [1997] 2001). Indeed, the notion that too much television can be bad for children continues to be a concern of the public and government.

In the 1970s there was a crisis in audience research around the notion of powerful media and powerful audience. In *The Effects of Television* (1970) James Halloran argued that 'we should ask not what the media does to people, but what people do to the media' (see www. museum.tv/archives/etv/T/htmlT/televisionst/televisionst.htm), which refocused an approach to the media and studying audiences. In 1974 Jay G. Blumler and Elihu Katz published a collection of essays that illustrated what they saw as a 'coming of age' of the 'uses and gratifications' approach. The opening chapter, taken from a paper given by Blumler, Katz and Gurevitch entitled 'Utilization of mass communication by the individual', both summarises the successes of the uses and gratifications approach and gestures towards future uses (1974: 13). In particular they draw on research by McQuail, Blumler and Brown (1972) on 'the television audience', who outlined the following categories:

> *diversion* (including escape from the constraints of routine and the burdens of problems, and emotional release); *personal relationships* (including substitute companionship as well as social utility); *personal identity* (including personal reference, reality exploration, and value reinforcement); and *surveillance*. (Blumler et al. 1974: 23, author's italics)

These categories are often used in media and audience textbooks to typify the 'uses and gratifications' approach. The central idea is that mass communication is used by individuals to connect to others (ibid.: 23).

Blumler and Katz's uses and gratifications theory was embraced by theorists such as John Fiske who argued that it assumes an active audience and implies that a message is what the audience makes of it ([1982] 1990: 151). However, other theorists have argued that it can appear rather simplistic and crude when compared to the complexity of how the audience/reader work with the text (see in particular Morley 1992: 52–4). One of the criticisms of uses and gratifications theory is that it implies that the media is capable of knowing what audiences want and is therefore able to give it to them. As Greg Philo argues in *Seeing & Believing: The Influence of Television*: 'this model does not come to terms with the complexity either of what is being transmitted by the media or the cultures within which the messages are being received' (1990: 6). Interrogating the way messages are received and the way in which media power is used formed the basis of the Glasgow Media Research Group, which undertook a range of studies into audience reception from industrial disputes, AIDS, 'mad cow disease' and the conflict in Northern Ireland (Kitzinger 1999: 4). 'One of the most common findings across all the projects is people's impressive ability to recall certain aspects of media reporting' and the revelation that 'at the most basic level, the mass media (news reports, soap opera, films) are clearly used as common reference points to explain or justify certain points of view' (Kitzinger 1999: 5). The Glasgow Media Group's research enables a more nuanced approach to the complexity of audience reception and the influence and power of the media (see Eldridge 1995; and Philo 1995).

Raymond Williams's work on television is often remembered through the term 'flow' which he used to describe the television watching experience. However, as Lynn Spigel points out in her introduction to the 1992 publication of *Television: Technology and Cultural Form* (org. pub. 1974), Williams's analysis of 'flow' is just one chapter in a 'throughgoing critique of the relationships among television's technological invention, its innovation as a media institution and textual form, and its connection to social relationships and experience in modern Western culture' (1992: x). Indeed, Williams's work on television, which includes his selected writings on television (1989) and his columns in *The Listener*, comprise a significant contribution to the study of television and its audiences. In his chapter on 'Programming: distribution and flow', Williams describes the 'interruptions' inherent to the television watching experience, but also notes the 'flow' that happens when programmes and advertisements begin to merge together on television. Williams saw this 'flow' as something distinct to American television and recounts the following experience of watching television in Miami, after arriving on an Atlantic liner: 'A crime in San Francisco (the subject of the original film) began to operate in an extraordinary counterpoint not only with the deodorant and cereal commercials but with a romance in Paris and the eruption of a prehistoric monster who laid waste New York' (Williams 1992 [1974]: 85–6). Here Williams refers to the way in which television programmes and advertisements 'flow' together even though there are breaks in the programming schedule, which, for Williams, results in 'a single irresponsible flow of images and feelings' (1992 [1974]: 86). In other words, because the programmes and advertisements share similar styles and content, the entire experience produces a 'flow' of feelings that are not always linked to any one programme or advertisement in particular. Williams's analysis of television's 'flow' poses interesting questions for studying emotion and television. Mark Jancovich and James Lyons argue, for instance, that:

> While television has traditionally been discussed in terms of habitual viewing and televisual 'flow' (Williams 1974), the trends . . . suggest that contemporary television has witnessed the emergence of 'must see TV', shows that are not simply part of a habitual flow of television programming but, either through design or audience response, have become 'essential viewing'. (2003: 2)

'Must see TV' or 'appointment viewing' has changed the way in which viewers watch television and, arguably, the way they both critically and emotionally judge what they watch.

However, with many viewers now watching television on the internet or on DVD, 'Must see TV' no longer has the same draw it once did. Indeed this is one of the problems the television industry faces. At the 2008 Console-ing Passions Conference, Dana Walden, Chair of Twentieth-Century Fox Television, discussed the difficulties in getting viewers to watch television when it is aired, rather than through other viewing practices. This change means that Williams's concept of 'flow' needs to be reconsidered to include these new viewing practices and relationships to feelings and images.

In his influential 'encoding-decoding' model (2001 [1980]), Stuart Hall brings new understanding to the ways in which audiences make sense of what they watch. He uses the example of an historical event to explain that it cannot be simply transmitted as a television broadcast, but instead, 'must become a "story" before it can become a *communicative event*' (Hall 2001 [1980]: 167, author's italics). He focuses his attention on the way in which messages are 'encoded' by television producers and 'decoded' by their audiences, noting that '[un]less they are wildly aberrant, encoding will have the effect of constructing some of the limits and parameters within which decodings will operate' (2001 [1980]: 173). Hall thus points the way to the study of interpretation before that of effect or impact:

> Before this message can have an 'effect' (however defined), satisfy a 'need' or be put to a 'use,' it must first be appropriated as meaningful discourse and be meaningfully decoded. It is this set of decoded meanings which 'have an effect,' influence, entertain, instruct or persuade, with very complex perceptual, cognitive, emotional, ideological or behavioural consequences. (2001 [1980]: 168)

Hall identifies three ways in which audiences may decode a text:

- **Dominant-hegemonic position**: 'where the viewer takes the connoted meaning from, say, a television newscast or current affairs programme full and straight, and decodes the message in terms of the reference code in which it has been encoded' (2001 [1980]: 174);
- **Negotiated code**: 'a mixture of adaptive and oppositional elements: it acknowledges the legitimacy of the hegemonic definitions to make the grand significations (abstract), while, at a more restricted, situational (situated) level, it makes it own ground rules – it operates with exceptions to the rule' (2001 [1980]: 175);
- **Oppositional code**: 'This is the case of the viewer who listens to a debate on the need to limit wages but "reads" every mention of the "national interest" as "class interest"' (2001 [1980]: 175).

In his work on audiences, Andy Ruddock uses the popular example of the film *Top Gun* (1987) to illustrate the 'dislocations' that can occur between encoding and decoding. For Douglas Kellner, *Top Gun*'s preferred meanings are clear: '*Top Gun*'s ideological project is to invest desire in the figure of the heroic fighter pilots and high tech war which it does with attractive star figures, cinematic high tech wizardry and special effects' (Kellner 1995, cited in Ruddock 2001: 124). However, Ruddock notes that his students do not see this preferred reading, rather they read *Top Gun* as a parody of masculinity and the 'USA #1' ethos (2001: 125). Indeed, there are many scenes that can be read as 'queer' – certainly not a reading intended by the producers. Ruddock points out that 'Asking whether the audience accepts or rejects a text's version of reality is fine when dealing with overtly political programming such as news or current affairs, but these criteria might be less relevant in other contexts' (2001: 148). However, the codes Hall identifies allow those interested in the study of audiences to consider the various ways in which audiences interpret what they watch and to appreciate the complexity inherent to the relationship between viewer and screen.

Following Hall's work, Charlotte Brunsdon and David Morley's work on *Nationwide* (1978) and Morley's subsequent work on the *Nationwide Audience* (1980) brought new attention to 'the social dimensions of viewing and interpretation' to audience studies (see Hall 1986:7). In his 'critical postscript' to the project (1992) Morley expands on his earlier ideas and identifies some crucial problems with the encoding/decoding model which informed his work. He argues for three major points of difficulty:

1. the slide towards intentionality;
2. the notion of television as a conveyor-belt for a pre-given message or 'meaning' rather than an understanding of the production of meaning in and through practices of signification;
3. the blurring of what are probably better conceived of as separate processes under the heading of 'decoding'. (1992: 120)

These are important interventions both into Hall's work and into Morley's own analysis of the audience. Some argue that Morley's 'critical postscript' marked the end of Hall's encoding/decoding research (Buckingham 1999, cited in Ruddock 2001: 149) while others, including Morley, suggest that this overlooks the importance Hall's work continues to have within television studies.

Another important body of work on audiences was advanced by Ien Ang in *Watching Dallas* (1985). Ang put the following advertisement in a women's magazine in Holland asking for views about the popular American television series *Dallas*: 'I like watching the TV serial *Dallas*, but often get odd reactions to it. Would anyone like to write and tell me why you like watching it too, or dislike it? I should like to assimilate these reactions in my university thesis. Please write to . . . ' (1985: 10). Part of what Ang's research reveals is the polysemic nature of television texts in that they can have a variety of meanings and that the audience is an important component in determining that meaning, something Chapter 2 will explore in more detail. But perhaps most importantly, Ang considered the role of *pleasure* in viewers' television watching experiences. Given that people are not forced to watch television, Ang considered 'the *mechanisms* by which pleasure is aroused' (1985: 9, author's italics). This leads Ang to appreciate how important characters, the fictional world they inhabit (and how real/unreal it is) and genre are in thinking about why people watch what they watch.

If we return to the distinctions drawn between theatre, film and television audiences at the beginning of this chapter, we are reminded that television has to compete much more than cinema and theatre with other distractions, other channels, other activities in the home, and one of the ways they do this is through the manner of their mode of address, the manner in which they try to involve us the audience/reader.

Generations of audience research

So far this chapter has considered the development of audience reception theory by citing influential models chronologically – however, this is just one way to tell the story of audience research. In *Audiences* (1998) Nicholas Abercrombie and Brian Longhurst suggest that: 'Typically, histories of audience research in the media divide up that history into phases, or periods. As far as television and radio are concerned, a common analysis is of three phases – "effects", "uses and gratifications", and "encoding/decoding"' (1998: 4). Similarly, in *Rethinking the Media Audience* (1999), Pertti Alasuutari examines developments in audience research in terms of phases, which offers another way of thinking about the progression of ideas on the audience. Alasuutari uses the notion of phases loosely, which enables us to think more broadly about the changes that have happened and the future of audience research.

Alasuutari dates the first phase of reception research to Stuart Hall's first attempts to think through encoding/decoding in 'Encoding and Decoding in the Television Discourse' (1974) and argues that from the beginning audience research in the UK was associated with the Centre for Contemporary Cultural Studies in Birmingham. However, as Alasuutari points out, 'when compared to earlier communication models (e.g. Gerbner 1956; Lasswell 1948; Shannon and Weaver 1963), Hall's encoding/decoding model is actually not a very radical change' (Alasuutari 1999: 3). Crucially, what Hall's work stressed was that messages were no longer understood as 'some kind of package or ball' (1999: 3) that was thrown at the audiences and 'caught'. Also important is to consider how Hall moves from an interpretation based on behavioural models to one that is more linguistically based and reliant on an interpretative framework. So instead of thinking about what people did with the messages or how it might effect them, Hall's model moved audience research into thinking about interpretation and analysis of messages on television: on the thought and meaning-making process. Hall's work led to a series of empirical studies on audience, most notably to David Morley's *Nationwide Audience* (1980), discussed earlier.

Morley's research was soon followed by further studies – particularly on the romantic serials, in what Alasuutari sees as the second generation of audience research. Ang's *Watching Dallas* (1985) was part of a broader interest in recuperating feminine forms. In *The Feminist, the Housewife and the Soap Opera* (2000a), Charlotte Brunsdon refers to this phase of feminist television criticism as 'reinvestigation'. Brunsdon proposes a 'repudiation-reinvestigation-revaluation' schema to characterise 'the relationship between second-wave feminism and mass cultural feminine forms' (2000a: 21). Her schema offers a very useful way of thinking about the development of feminist television criticism, which included work on soap operas such as Dorothy Hobson's *Crossroads: The Drama of a Soap Opera* (1982). Hobson's work is also illustrative of a shift in television audience research towards ethnography. As Alasuutari notes, researchers were now analysing a programme and studying its reception through focus groups and interviews.

Alasuutari dates the third generation back to the 1980s when theorists began to question and critique ethnographic work. Most importantly they began to question the notion of an audience (see also Burton 2000: 211–32). This generation also thought about the place of the media in everyday life, evident in work such as S. Elizabeth Bird's *The Audience in Everyday Life* (2003). In this phase of audience research, ethnography is not completely thrown out; instead of trying to understand the audience, theorists now use ethnography to have a sense of contemporary media culture. This focus on ethnography also added an element of reflexivity in that it also asked the audience to reflect on themselves as audience and as a researcher (see Carolyn Ellis, *The Ethnographic 'I'* [2004]). For instance, Ellen Seiter critically discusses a case of a 'troubling' interview where the respondents talked more about high culture than soaps (the focus of the interview) because they felt intimidated by her status as an academic. As Seiter argues: 'Television watching can be a touchy subject . . . This interview exemplifies the defensiveness that men and women unprotected by academic credentials may feel in admitting to television viewing in part because of its connotations of feminine passivity, laziness and vulgarity' (2000: 496). Seiter recognised that her position as an academic made it difficult for her interviewees to discuss their television watching experiences candidly. Instead they felt they needed to justify their own intellectual interests and downplay their television watching.

Alasuutari summarises the three generations he identifies as follows: 'interpretive communities', ethnographic turn and reflection on the everyday (1999: 6–7). They are informed by Foucault's influence on discourse theory (poststructuralism), feminist theory and theories into fan cultures, and, perhaps most importantly to this chapter, as seeing the audience as active. This process of making meaning is what makes television a polysemic medium. That is, it comprises many signs, generated through a variety of codes: visual, verbal, technical, nonverbal and so on. As Burton argues in *Talking Television*: 'Sitting still is not the same thing as being inactive' (2000: 215).

New developments in audience research

The final section of this chapter will introduce some recent developments in audience research as a way of posing new questions about the audience and enticing you to read more about the study of audience reception. Anna McCarthy's 'television while you wait' and recent research on reality TV are just two examples of the new directions audience research is taking and illustrate ideas important to a theorisation of emotion and television.

'Television while you wait'
In *Ambient Television: Visual Culture and Public Space*, Anna McCarthy considers '[w]hat the TV set *does* outside the home – what social acts it performs, or is roped into, what struggles it embodies and intervenes in, what agencies speak through it, and which subjects it silences or alternatively gives a voice' (2001: 1, author's italics). In so doing, she poses very provocative questions about the presence of television

in the public domain. McCarthy also critiques the notion of 'dead' time and considers how TV becomes a way for us to kill time or to consume something while we wait for the next activity. This notion can be applied to moments in waiting rooms, airports, restaurants, or even at home. McCarthy draws on work in sociology to suggest that public spaces are divided between those who have to wait and those who do not. Television's role in this waiting often signifies the activity as passive. And yet, McCarthy argues that the act of watching while waiting can sometimes make a viewer feel as though she passed the time meaningfully. As she argues: 'Often associated with *wasting* time, watching television is a way of passing time suddenly *legitimized* when it takes place in waiting environments' (2001: 199, author's italics). So if we return to the powerful media/powerful viewer debate discussed earlier in this chapter – we can recognise in McCarthy's argument the desire to save television from being seen as a passive activity, as it is so often constructed, and instead to identify a sense of activity in the process of watching TV – *even* while waiting for something else to happen.

McCarthy's interest in 'ambient television' leads her to questions regarding television audiences. For instance, she asks:

> How much is the experience of waiting built into the format of TV programming and images in general – waiting for an upcoming program, a better music video, the resumption of a narrative interrupted by commercials? In other words, is waiting a 'deep structure' of television spectatorship regardless of where we watch TV? (2001: 218–19)

McCarthy's questions are important insofar as they remind us how often television is used by its viewers to pass time. Whether we are waiting in a doctor's office or for dinner to be ready, television is often available to deal with feelings of boredom or restlessness. These engagements are very seldom emotional and very often forgettable. Indeed, a good deal of the time spent in front of the television can be understood as meaningless.

And yet, as McCarthy points out, televisions are often situated in eating places to make people feel better about eating alone or to relieve their anxieties of wasting time. She mentions a place in Manhattan called The Video Diner which has individualised booths where you can watch TV and eat – and contrasts this with sports bars and news bars. She reminds us that we need to think about the 'material conventions of the screen as an object' (2001: 222); in other words, we need to think about how the physical position of the screen affects the spectator's experience of watching TV. Perhaps we can take this a step further to suggest that it is necessary to think about the viewer's orientation to the screen in order to make sense of their engagement with what they watch. The viewer in The Video Diner will have a very different commitment to a TV programme than the person in a sports bar, as will the person who sits down to watch a particular programme versus the one who tunes in while she waits. McCarthy's research generates significant questions about the television audience, the role of television in the public sphere and, important to this book, the way people engage with what they watch. This book is not suggesting that all moments spent in front of the television are emotional or meaningful, far from it. Rather, it is interested in how emotion functions in television and how the industry values it.

Questions for consideration:

- How often and where do you watch television 'while you wait'?
- What kind of watching are you doing? Is it different from when you are at home?
- What does McCarthy mean by 'commodify' the act of waiting?

Understanding reality TV

What is reality TV and why is it so difficult to define? These are the fundamental questions that underpin Holmes and Jermyn's collection on reality television entitled *Understanding Reality Television*.

In 2002, Friedman argued: 'As we embark upon a new century of broadcasting, it is clear that no genre form or type of programming has been as actively marketed by producers, or more enthusiastically embraced by viewers, than reality-based TV' (cited in Holmes and Jermyn 2004: 1). The rise in reality television emphasises, as Holmes and Jermyn argue: 'how the formats, images and conventions of Reality TV have stitched themselves into the very fabric of television, its economic structures, schedules and viewing cultures' (2004: 1).

In 1994, Kilborn tried to define reality TV and gave it the following characteristics:

- Recording 'on the wing', and frequently with the help of lightweight video equipment, of events in the lives of individuals and groups;
- The attempt to simulate such real-life events through various forms of dramatised reconstruction;
- The incorporation of this material in suitably edited form into an attractively packaged television programme which can be promoted on the strength of its reality credentials. (cited in Holmes and Jermyn 2004: 2)

As Kilborn points out, new technology, such as the invention of light-weight video cameras led to an increase in footage documenting people's everyday lives and to programmes such as *America's Funniest Home Videos* (ABC 1989) and the British version, *You've Been Framed* (ITV 1990–) which capitalise on this form of 'packaged' drama. Peter Bazalgette, creator of Endemol Productions (*Big Brother*) celebrates the impact of new technology on the reality format and points out that:

> *Big Brother* is one idea exploited across about nine different media using each medium for what it does best. So on Channel 4 – terrestrial television – there's a traditional, edited half-hour – a narrative documentary, if you like, of the previous twenty-four hours. On E4 – a digital channel – you could choose from four different options. Live streams from the house (delayed by ten minutes) or material from two and four hours ago. (2001: 2)

As Bazalgette suggests, part of the allure of the reality format is in its flexibility across the media – in its ability to be edited and reformatted to provide hours of entertainment to those willing to watch.

Restyling factual TV
Annette Hill defines reality TV, or popular factual TV, as 'a catch-all category for a variety of different one-off programmes, series or formats that follow real people and celebrities and their everyday or out of the ordinary experiences' (2007: 5). Hill's definition is useful and points towards her thesis that viewers make sense of reality television based on their understanding of other factual genres, namely, the news. As she explains: 'For audiences, news is the first, and still the most familiar, factual television genre, and in many ways all other factual genres are evaluated alongside viewers' understanding and experience of news' (2007: 4). Further, viewers use their understanding of factual television to make sense of the chaos that now defines reality television (2007: 2). As she points out, 'In a report by Ofcom on British TV in 2005, general factual (meaning all factual content that was not news or current affairs) was the largest growth genre' (2007: 6). The growth, popularity and continuing success of reality television makes it an unavoidable aspect for audience research. Interestingly for this work, Hill identifies an emotional engagement with reality based television and argues that: 'The focus on emotions has become a trademark for many factual programmes, where the premise is to observe or put people in emotionally difficult situations' (2007: 15). This notion of people being put in emotionally difficult situations will be explored in more detail in Chapter 7 in a case study on *Wife Swap* but can be

extended to cover many similar programmes that use this approach in order to engage the audience.

Case study: *Family Guy* (Fox 1999–)

One of the best examples of the way in which viewers have become more television literate can be found in the popular US animated comedy, *Family Guy*. Similar in many ways to *The Simpsons* but more irreverent and cynical, *Family Guy*'s inter-textual references to other television programmes, films and cultural events illustrate ways in which viewers today are expected to be able to read television faster than before. The programme's consistent and often frustrating use of cut-aways keeps the viewer active in the sense that he or she must follow the text as it veers through flashbacks, flash-forwards and other narrative devices aimed at disrupting a conventional (and even coherent) narrative. At the same time, it could be argued that the text demonstrates a lazy and impatient audience in that these narrative devices keep the viewer entertained. Instead of developing story lines, the programme can be accused of playing to the gallery in its attempts for a laugh. Consider ways in which this television programme implies an active and passive audience.

Note

1. See Noble 1975, as cited in Livingstone [1990] 1998: 15.

Discussion/Exercises

1. Consider one of the three examples of new research in audience reception ('Television while you wait'; Understanding reality TV; Restyling factual TV) and think about which earlier models have influenced it. Now consider what role emotion might play in these new models of audience reception.
2. Discuss the strengths and weaknesses of the audience models mentioned in this chapter. How else might researchers measure audience response?
3. Is the term 'audience' helpful when discussing television viewers? Can you think of a more useful term?

Further reading

Abercrombie, Nicholas and Brian Longhurst (1998), *Audiences*, London: Sage.

Adorno, Theodor (1991), *The Culture Industry: Selected Essays on Mass Culture*, ed. J. M. Bernstein, London: Routledge.

Adorno, Theodor and Max Horkheimer (1979), *Dialectic of Enlightenment*, London: Verso.

Alasuutari, Pertti (ed.) (1999), *Rethinking the Media Audience*, London: Sage.

Ang, Ien (1991), *Desperately Seeking the Audience*, London: Routledge.

Blumler, Jay G. and Elihu Katz (eds) (1974), *The Uses of Mass Communications: Current Perspectives on Gratifications Research*, Beverly Hills: Sage.

Brooker, Will and Deborah Jermyn (eds) (2003), *The Audience Studies Reader*, London: Routledge.

Brunsdon, Charlotte and David Morley (1978), *Everyday Television: Nationwide*, London: British Film Institute.

Eldridge, John (ed.) (1995), *Glasgow Media Group Reader; Volume 1: News Content, Language and Visuals*, London and New York: Routledge.

Halloran, James (1970), *The Effects of Television*, London: Panther.

Hill, Annette (2007), *Restyling Factual TV: Audiences and News, Documentary and Reality Genres*, London: Routledge.

Kitzinger, Jenny (1999), 'A sociology of media power: key issues in audience reception research', in Greg Philo (ed.), *Message Received*, Harlow: Longman, pp. 2–20.

Livingstone, Sonia ([1990] 1998), *Making Sense of Television: The Psychology of Audience Interpretation*, 2nd edn, London: Routledge.

Livingstone, Sonia and Peter Lunt (1994), *Talk on Television: Audience Participation and Public Debate*, London: Routledge.

MacCarthy, Anna (2001), *Ambient Television: Visual Culture and Public Space*, Durham, NC: Duke University Press.

Moores, Shaun (1993), *Interpreting Audiences: The Ethnography of Media Consumption*, London: Sage.

Morley, David (1980), *The Nationwide Audience*, London: British Film Institute.

Nightingale, Virginia (1996), *Studying Audiences: The Shock of the Real*, London: Routledge.

Philo, Greg and David Miller (eds) (2001), *Market Killing: What the Free Market Does and What Social Scientists Can Do about It*, Essex: Pearson Education.

Philo, Greg (ed.) (1999), *Message Received: Glasgow Media Group Research, 1993–1998*, Harlow Longman.

— (ed.) (1995) *Glasgow Media Group Reader; Volume 2: Industry, Economy, War and Politics*, London and New York: Routledge.

Philo, Greg (1990), *Seeing and Believing: The Influence of Television*, London and New York: Routledge.

Ross, Karen and Virginia Nightingale (2003), *Media and Audiences: New Perspectives*, Maidenhead: Open University Press.

Seiter, Ellen (2000), 'Making distinctions in TV audience research: case study of a troubling interview', in Horace Newcomb (ed.), *Television: The Critical View*, Oxford: Oxford University Press, pp. 495–518.

Useful web links

http://flowtv.org
http://www.gla.ac.uk/centres/mediagroup/index.htm
www.criticalstudiesintelevision.com
www.participations.org

2 Personal Meanings, Fandom and Sitting Too Close to the Television

What are the requirements for transforming a book or a movie into a cult object? The work must be loved, obviously, but this is not enough. It must provide a completely furnished world so that its fans can quote characters and episodes as if they were aspects of the fan's private sectarian world . . . I think that in order to transform a work into a cult object one must be able to break, dislocate, unhinge it so that one can remember only parts of it, irrespective of their original relationship with the whole.

(Eco 1986: 197–8, cited in Jenkins 1992: 50)

Henry Jenkins explains the way 'texts become real' by recalling the moment in *The Velveteen Rabbit* (1983) when the Skin Horse tells the Rabbit that "'Real isn't how you are made. It's a thing that happens to you. When a child loves you for a long, long time, not just to play with, but REALLY loves you, then you become real'" (Bianco 1983: 4, cited in Jenkins 1992: 50). A more contemporary example can be found in *Toy Story 2* (2000) when Woody (Tom Hanks) believes he is truly loved because his child owner has put his initials on the sole of his foot. Indeed, when the toymaker paints over these initials, in an effort to 'repair' him and thus increase his collectable value, Woody feels truly lost for the first time. The marks on a well-loved toy represent signs of love and attachment in a similar way turned-down pages and a broken spine might indicate affection for a favourite book. But how does a viewer make a television text real (or show her love)? Part of the suggestion in Jenkins's *Textual Poachers* (1992) and other work in fan cultures is that a viewer makes the text real (or demonstrates her love) through knowledge of the text and fan production, which may include any number of activities from songs to blogs to 'you tube' re-edited episodes. The fan's practice of taking the text and adding to it marks it in a way similar to the actions of an adoring child or a devoted reader. However, these loving practices are also part of the reason the fan is associated with immaturity and an inability to distinguish between reality and fiction. Indeed, the sentimental attachment demonstrated by the fan is perceived as an uncritical and even unhealthy relationship by some and yet validated and supported by others. Instead of taking on the well-rehearsed debates between powerful fans and powerful producers – which essentially maps itself onto the debate between powerful media and powerful audience discussed in the last chapter – this chapter will focus on the meaning fans/readers/critics give to particular television texts, the affective dimensions of this 'meaning-making', and consider a way to rethink the 'dangers' of 'sitting too close to the tele'.

How do we make sense of what we watch?

In his excellent study *Making Meaning: Inference and Rhetoric in the Interpretation of Cinema*, David Bordwell draws a distinction between comprehending a film and interpreting it (1989: 2). Bordwell refers to the Bond movies and argues that while most viewers can follow the plot not everyone will be able to appreciate the ideological, psycho-sexual or symbolic significance of the film. He explains that 'Roughly speaking, one can understand the plot of a James Bond film while remaining wholly oblivious to its more abstract mythic, religious, ide-ological, or psychosexual significance' (1989: 2). Indeed, many viewers will watch Bond films as entertainment while at the same time, as a collection such as *The James Bond Phenomenon* (Lindner 2003) or *Violent Femmes: Women as Spies in Popular Culture* (White 2007) dem-onstrates, others will read the films as symptomatic of cultural shifts and analyse them in terms of critical theory. Using the example of Bond films, Bordwell draws out the way there are hidden meanings or levels of meaning, as he explains: 'meanings are not found but made' (1989: 3). In other words, Bordwell argues that the viewer brings meaning to the text and in so doing derives pleasure from this kind of meaning-making. He argues that: 'Criticism certainly gives pleasure to its practitioners. It yields the intellectual satisfaction of problem-solving, the delight of coming to know a loved artwork more fully, the mastery of a skill, the security of belonging to a community' (1989: 40). The 'textual production,' as Fiske refers to it (1992: 30), that fans make is a labour of love and one that involves an active interest in renegotiat-ing the meanings within and beyond a particular text.

Bordwell's understanding of the way critics love to make meaning of their texts shares similarities with Michel de Certeau's work in *The Practice of Everyday Life* (1984). In his chapter on 'reading as poaching', de Certeau begins with the dismissal of readers as passive and submissive; he argues that reading has been re-understood as not just taking the meaning given, but adding to it – so much so that someone (i.e. a literary critic) might come up with a different meaning altogether. De Certeau is critical of the education system that denies students the 'authority' to come up with their own readings and are always encouraged to take the accepted reading instead – steered back to the 'right' answer (1984: 173). He forces us to think about *who* is reading and how our bodies are orientated towards that reading. For example, de Certeau suggests we pay attention to the body's movements when reading in reading rooms and we can extend this to think about the way we watch television in domestic spaces (1984: 175). Or, as discussed in Chapter 1, we can think about the place of television in the public sphere and how we might 'read' the television differently depending on where we are watching it.

De Certeau's work is part of a broader interest in the 'everyday'. In his work on media, technology and everyday life, Hermann Bausinger claims that 'today everybody talks about the everyday, even the empiricists' (1984: 343). What was once an inconspicuous concept, became in the 1980s a very conspicuous one and although phrased in different ways, such as, 'the consciousness of the everyday, knowledge of the everyday, culture of the everyday, behaviour of the everyday' (1984: 343) 'everyday' was used as a way of drawing interest in people's daily routines and experiences. As Bausinger suggests, the 'everyday' is crucial in our study of the media, particularly television and its audiences, and how people make meaning from the media around them. In order to think about this further, we must first think about the variety of media that people encounter from the moment they wake until the end of their day. So, for instance, the radio or a cell phone might be the first form of media someone encounters and, perhaps, the last. The images, sound bites and memorable melodies that confront us as we rush through our daily routines will inevitably find their way into the meanings we make whether about the weather, our lives or an event across the world.

Interpersonal forms of media, such as television, are integrated into people's daily lives. Many families, for example, have televisions in their kitchens and/or bedrooms, as well as in the main family room. This means that the television often becomes a backdrop, as well as a focal point, in people's everyday lives. As a social tool and as something with varied content, television is something people talk about, whether in groups, over the 'watercooler', or on online forums. Chat rooms dedicated to particular programmes now offer 'webisodes' or 'mobisodes' to further a viewer's interest in a particular television programme. The consequences of this are a further engagement with television and its various media outputs.

The emphasis on the 'everyday' and 'meaning' was taken up in television studies in the 1990s, particularly in Roger Silverstone's *Television and Everyday Life* (1994) and Sonia Livingstone's *Making Sense of Television: The Psychology of Audience Interpretation* (1998 [1990]). As Livingstone argues,

> All day, every day, people create and recreate meanings in their everyday lives. Whether they are working, talking to their children, watching television, judging the weather, planning a meal or playing a record, people routinely and apparently unproblematically make sense of the circumstances. (1998: 4)

And yet, as Livingstone also points out, this meaning making is far from straightforward or unproblematic. Indeed, it is near impossible to pin down the meanings audiences take from what they watch or to separate meanings taken from television and those taken from everyday life.

David Gauntlett and Annette Hill continued this interest in the everyday and meaning through their ethnographic work in *TV Living* (1999). Gauntlett and Hill's book synthesises the findings of a British Film Institute project in which 500 participants completed detailed questionnaire-diaries over a five-year period, writing around three and a half million words on their lives, their television watching and the relationship between the two. Their work illustrates a shift towards empirical, ethnographic work – and the stress on powerful viewers – and in essence this project follows in the 'footsteps' of Morley's work (from *Nationwide Audience* [1980] study to *Family Television* [1986]) (Gauntlett and Hill 1999: 3). Gauntlet and Hill study the impact that gender, age, class, new technologies and domesticity have on viewers' understanding and appreciation of television. They also look at how families negotiate TV watching (obviously some families solve this by buying more TVs). They look at the impact new technologies, such as cable, have on viewing and address viewer's guilty or ambivalent feelings about television. The main premise – or the central theoretical framework they work within – is that television is part of everyday life. As Gauntlett and Hill's research demonstrates, people will often schedule their day around a particular programme. Although with the invention of digital recording systems and online streaming, 'appointment television' is increasingly outmoded. Centrally the notion is that TV is important to people – whether shared individually or publicly. Gauntlett and Hill break down some of the personal engagements as follows: 'electronic wallpaper', 'a good friend' and 'one of the family' (1999: 112–19). As one of their participants writes:

> Television is an important part of my life. I rarely have it on if there is nothing I want to watch, but if there is a good programme on I love sitting down to watch it with a cup of coffee and a bar of chocolate. Often I time my meals to coincide with something good. I like eating and watching television. I also often iron whilst watching. When I clean I prefer listening to music.' (24-year-old female electronic engineer) (Gauntlett and Hill 1999: 23)

As Gauntlett and Hill's research illustrates, television is often a significant part of people's everyday lives. It is integrated into the fabric of everyday rituals and, as such, becomes something essential to them.

Although television is often part of people's everyday lives and rituals, this does not necessarily mean that viewers are consistently making meaning out of what they watch. As discussed in the Introduction, there are times when viewers are passive, and times when they are active. In his conclusion to research carried out by the Glasgow Media Group, Greg Philo states that:

> It would be quite wrong to see audiences as simply absorbing all media messages, and certainly as being unable to distinguish between fact and fiction. But it is also wrong to see viewers and readers as effortlessly active, creating their own meanings in each encounter with the text. (1999a: 287)

For this reason, ethnographic work continues to be a vital way to study audiences and the meanings they make.

From everyday life to fandom

De Certeau's work also had a significant influence on how theorists considered the relationship between television and its fans. Indeed, the notion that fans actively read texts is reflected in Jenkins's title, *Textual Poachers: Television Fans and Participatory Culture* (1992). Jenkins borrows the term 'poaching' from Michel de Certeau's (1984) *The Practice of Everyday Life*.[1] Jenkins's work marked a change in previous research on fandom because he was a fan himself (of *Star Trek*). Where is the divide then between the fan and the critic? Perhaps unsurprisingly, this question is at the heart of both Henry Jenkins's and Matt Hills's work on fan cultures. Each devotes a lot of energy outlining the differences and similarities between the fan and the academic, in terms of their interest in fan cultures. Jenkins argues that

'There's an argument in semiotics that seems to imply that meaning can be derived from a text and then you throw the text away. The difference is fans don't throw the text away, that there's an emotional connection to the text that survives any generation of meaning from it. (2001)

As Jenkins suggests, meaning and emotion have a lot to do with television's legacy.

In Simon Pegg and Jessica Stevenson's critically acclaimed situation comedy *Spaced*[2] (Channel 4 2006) Daisy Steiner and Tim Bisley must pretend to be a couple in order to live together in a flat in London. As they run through their histories of each other Daisy asks Tim if he is one of those 'sci-fi nerds'. She asks him: 'You don't spend your evenings on the internet discussing symbolism in the *X-Files*?' To which he replies: 'Look, modern science fiction can be pretty interesting. The thoughts and speculations of our contemporary authors and thinkers have probably never been closer to the truth.' At which point the scene shifts and we see aliens jumping up and down and laughing in front of the shop where Tim works, appropriately called Fantasy Bazaar. The scene illustrates Hills's notion of the 'fans-as-intellectual'[3] and parodies the negative assumptions made of fandom. Tim's mock erudite reply also pokes fun of the academic rhetoric surrounding fan cultures and perpetuates the notion that fandom is a troubled activity.

And yet, new viewing practices, particularly the consumption of DVD box sets, has started to make a fan of many of us. Before arguing this point, I want to discuss the position of the fan, as much of the literature on fandom focuses on the ways in which we personalise and make meaning out of what we watch on television. The pleasure of 'meaning making' underlines the experience of the fan – the fan can unpick, unravel and reveal the secret meanings of a text and produce her own online which secures her place within a community and as an expert of a particular text. As Fiske argues:

All popular audiences engage in varying degrees of semiotic productivity, producing meanings and pleasures that pertain to their social situation out of the products of the culture industries. But fans often turn this semiotic productivity into some form of textual production that can circulate among – and thus help to define – the fan community. (1992: 30)

As Jenkins reminds us, the word 'fan', short for 'fanatic', 'has its roots in the Latin word "fanaticus" which means "of or belonging to the temple, a temple servant, a devotee"' (1992: 12). The word itself underscores the way a fan is devoted to or obsessed by a particular text.

And here it might be important to distinguish between a fan, a cultist and an enthusiast, since many of these terms are often conflated. However, as Hills usefully argues, 'rigorous definitions' of 'fan' and 'cult' are not productive. He points out that, in fixing the terms of reference between 'cult' and 'fandom', 'these types of argument neglect to consider that terms such as "fan" and "cult" may not circulate simply as "labels" for actual things or referents, but may instead form part of a cultural struggle over meaning and affect' (2002: xi). To insist on concrete definitions overlooks the passions and attachments a fan might have for a text and misses the way in which some self-identifying fans still have problems with the term itself. Hills also reminds us that being a fan is often performative, so to limit and constrict this performance will inevitably miss the interactivity and ingenuity noted within fan cultures.

What sort of series are objects of fandom? As Henry Jenkins explains in *Textual Poachers* (1992), fans are often fans of science fiction television, programmes such as: *Alien Nation*; *The Avengers*; *Batman*; *Battlestar Galactica*; *Blake's 7*; *Doctor Who*; *Quantum Leap*; *Red Dwarf*; *Star Trek*; and *Twin Peaks*. But people can also be fans of programmes such as *Sex and the City*, *The Sopranos*, *The Wire*, *Lost* and *24* – and indeed, the television industry has begun to capitalise on fandom by offering 'webisodes', 'mobisodes', computer games and other commodified forms of fandom.

Although Jenkins did not intend *Textual Poachers* to become a 'unified theory of fandom' (2001), his work continues to be a significant point of reference for subsequent research on fan cultures. Jenkins catalogues some of the popular stereotypes of the fan. For instance, he suggests that people often think fans:

1. 'are brainless consumers who will buy anything associated with the program or its cast';
2. 'devote their lives to the cultivation of worthless knowledge';
3. 'place inappropriate importance on devalued cultural material';
4. 'are social misfits who have become so obsessed with the show that it forecloses other types of social experience';
5. 'are feminised and/or desexualised through their intimate engagement with mass culture';
6. 'are infantile, emotionally and intellectually immature';
7. 'are unable to separate fantasy from reality'. (1992: 10)

Jenkins's list exposes the way in which fans' emotional, intellectual and personal choices are attacked by virtue of their choice of television programme. There is a sense that this person is unable to have a healthy relationship to the text and therefore becomes an object of ridicule. What is interesting with regards to this book is the notion that the fan is emotionally immature and this is supported by the idea that the fan only develops emotional relationships with fictional characters and not 'real' people. Jenkins argues, however, that 'fans recognise that their relationship to the text remains a tentative one, that their pleasures often exist on the margins of the original text and in the face of the producer's own efforts to regulate its meanings' (1992: 24). While fans may demonstrate a strong attachment to certain texts they are also aware that they are not their own – they do not belong to them: they know that someone else has the power to do things to the characters they have grown to love (1992: 24).

Films and television programmes have played with culturally constructed notions of fandom and often represent the fan as someone who is out of touch with reality and lost in the fictional world of his or her fandom. Stephen King's *Misery* (Reiner 1990), for instance, brilliantly demonstrates the negative associations of fandom through the portrayal of a fan's obsessive need to control the ending of one of her favourite characters. When she finds out that the man she has saved from a car accident is the novelist of her favourite romance series, she holds him prisoner, forcing him to write the story she wants to read. In this example, Annie Wilkes (Kathy Bates) perfectly illustrates the negative stereotypes within popular culture of a fan – of someone who is not emotionally developed, is obsessively stuck in the world of her favourite text (fiction) and who does not have healthy relationships with other people in the world. In contrast, *Galaxy Quest* (Parisot 1999) begins with the negative associations of fan cultures but ends with a celebration of fandom and its knowledge. The film begins at a fan conference for a popular science fiction television series called *Galaxy Quest* (modelled after *Star Trek*). The actors are asked to appear at the conference and their reticence and frustration with what they perceive of as 'losers' recalls *Star Trek* star William Shatner's (Captain James T. Kirk) appearance on *Saturday Night Live* when he told a crowd of mock fans: "'Get a Life, will you people? I mean, I mean, for crying out loud, it's just a TV show!'" (cited in Jenkins 1992: 10). However, when the actors are abducted by aliens and reality and fiction are confused, the actors must rely on the fans' expert knowledge to save themselves. In this example, those sceptical of fandom re-evaluate and even celebrate the knowledge of the fan. The film usefully demonstrates the 'positive' and active aspects of fandom that Jenkins outlines in *Textual Poachers*.

Some argue that Jenkins's work on fandom is too celebratory. However, as Hills points out: 'Jenkins's work therefore needs to be viewed not simply as an example of academic-fan hybridity, but also as a rhetorical tailoring of fandom in order to act upon particular academic institutional spaces and agendas' (2002: 10). Jenkins himself points out that despite explaining how little power fans have, giving them any has resulted in this 'celebratory' label (2001). Not all critics are as positive about fandom as Jenkins. For instance, in *Understanding Audiences* (2001) Andy Ruddock argues that:

> While most of us manage to break free of such trivia [Posh and Becks] from time to time to consider more weighty matters, fans spend all their time pursuing such social relationships. What is worse, the people whom they pursue are often not even real. Fans are, in short, ultimate victims of realism as textual practice; people who are entirely convinced by media artifice. (2001: 154)

Ruddock's criticism reiterates the stereotypes and negative associations Jenkins identifies: that of a person who is emotionally immature and unable to distinguish fiction from reality. This critique of fandom stands in opposition to Jenkins's work which only serves to construct an 'either/or' debate. As Mark Jancovich and James Lyons argue: '[it] is important to recognise that in rejecting the romanticisation of the fan in Cultural Studies, there is always a risk of simply inverting the problem, and presenting the fan as consumer dupe' (2003: 7). They advise examining not only the encounter between fans and media texts but also the interaction between fans themselves; as they point out: '[f] ans or fan practices are not all the same' (2003: 7).

Sitting too close to the tele[4]

Many of us will remember being warned not to sit too close to the television when we were growing up. In *Textual Poachers* (1992) Jenkins suggests that this warning about closeness is also related to formulations of critical distance and aesthetics. Drawing on Bourdieu and Brecht, Jenkins reminds us that 'bourgeois aesthetics' value distance over proximity – one must be able to stand back and appreciate something in order to recognise its aesthetic value. This valuation of critical distance is also evident in film theory, where Christian Metz (1975) and Mary Ann Doane (1991) have placed value on distance, arguing that emotional closeness disables the viewer of being critically evaluative.

As I have argued elsewhere (Gorton 2008a), this viewpoint needs to be challenged for a number of reasons. First, as Jenkins convincingly argues, what critics such as Doane miss is that 'only by close engagement with its meanings and materials can fans fully consume the fiction and make it an active resource' (1992: 62). Secondly, recent work on emotion, which will be discussed in more detail in Chapter 4, fundamentally challenges the notion that knowledge is gained solely through rational distance and has substantiated the place of emotion in rational decision making. What is important here is to trouble the either/or position this debate constructs. Why do we have to have distance or closeness? Why can we not be savvy enough to understand that: (1) viewers can be critical of texts they are emotionally involved in; and (2) viewers are not always either distant or close – sometimes they are indifferent, bored, and/or uninterested. In *The Wow Climax: Tracing the Emotional Impact of Popular Culture* (2007) Jenkins argues that:

> Most popular culture is shaped by a logic of emotional intensification. It is less interested in making us think than it is in making us feel. Yet that distinction is too simple: popular culture, at its best, makes us think by making us feel. (2007: 3)

Jenkins's point is crucial in so far as it questions a lazy assumption that in feeling we are not thinking and instead posits the notion that emotions facilitate our intellect and choices.

In his lecture on 'broadcast television and the social contract', Thomas Elsaesser argues that: 'desire when watching TV becomes manageable and meaningful by making not morons, but specialists of us all' (1992: 14). He refers to the ways in which we watch for the smallest details in order to confirm our knowledge of a programme or character. He goes on to suggests that:

> we watch in the endlessly renewable hope that politicians and celebrities will give us the 'psychopathology of public life', when a momentary hesitation, a sideways look, an unguarded gesture, an awkward stride will unmask them as impersonators and impostors, catch them out as players and performers. (1992: 14)

Elsaesser's suggestion that desire comes through in the ways in which viewers want to know the intimate details of television's content can be linked to activities within fan cultures. We can theorise emotion in television in terms of the ways in which viewers gain knowledge about the intimate lives of their favourite soap characters, reality show participants or talk show guests. The desire for the details of these characters functions in a similar way to the process of getting to know a beloved (and we can extend this theorisation to think about why people enjoy celebrity magazines). It reiterates the suggestion made by contemporary theorists that we are living in an increasingly isolated and alienated society – where people look for intimacy on screen (whether on television, the internet, film) instead of finding it in other people and where fandom is no longer something carried out in the dark recesses of the imagination but in the public domain.

We must also consider the gaze that is involved in television watching – we must think about how close we get to the television in literal/physical terms. Previous research suggested that the televisual gaze was very different from the cinematic gaze. John Ellis has argued that 'TV is more about the look, and the glance and sound' than the cinematic gaze (cited in Moore 1989: 50). However with the increase in DVD box sets and digital recording devices (such as TiVo) we must question whether viewers are watching more intensely than a look or a glance. Indeed, the popularity of television programmes such as *Sex and the City* suggest that their audiences are watching with an intense gaze and that they might often rewatch episodes (or seasons) on DVD. Although a televisual glance still exists, there is an emergent gaze that is more intense and, I would argue, one filled with an emotional engagement. In his influential *Televisuality*, John Caldwell argues that Ellis's 'glance theory' is not an adequate 'description of emergent televisuality' (Caldwell 1995: 25). Nelson argues that

> More people perhaps now watch alone, or in a more concentrated way with others, perhaps with the lights dimmed, isolating selected texts and focusing upon the screen image. The dominant viewing mode, if not quite familiar, probably remains collective and domestic in small groups, perhaps of friends, in a lit space promoting talk about the programme as it is being aired. (2007: 15)

Jenkins has also pointed out that because of different viewing practices, people are watching more than one episode, returning to specific scenes, paying attention to backstory: '[t]he result is a televisual text much denser in narrative opportunities for fans than before; it has been designed to accommodate fan-fiction reading, not treat fan-fiction reading as some sort of opposition imposed on the text from the outside' (2001). Matt Hills argues that the rise in DVD box sets has meant that certain programmes have become more akin to 'artworks or novels' (2007: 4). Popular television programmes such as *Lost* or *24* are designed with the fan-watcher in mind – and the corresponding material that goes along with the programme online works to keep the viewer engaged in the programme between episodes or series. Derek Johnson reiterates this viewpoint in suggesting that: 'Audiences are not just cultivated as fans, but also *invited in*, asked to participate in both the world of the television text and the processes of its production' (2007: 63). Drawing on *Lost* and *24*, Johnson illustrates the ways in which 'spatial relationships of consumers, texts and production have been reconfigured' (2007: 63). Changes in programmes and the way they are produced and marketed has had a significant influence on the way people watch television and engage with it emotionally.

In her essay on 'Resistance, Online Fandom and Studio Censorship', Sara Gwenllian-Jones argues that:

> Distinctions between the so-called 'general audience' and so-called 'fandom' have become increasingly blurred as cult series become franchises; today, shops such as Forbidden Planet selling series-related merchandises can be found on the high streets of most provincial cities, catering not to hardcore fans but to a mainstream market that increasingly resembles fandom. (2003: 165)

Television has historically played a role in mass consumerism, particularly through advertising; but now with the internet and shops such as Forbidden Planet there is an emergent market that caters and indeed fosters a new kind of fandom.

Lawrence Grossberg's work on fandom illustrates a move within cultural theory towards understanding the affective relationship fans have with their beloved texts. In his essay on the 'indifference of television' (1987), for instance, following Ellis's assertion of a 'glance', Grossberg argued that the 'in-difference' of television 'makes the very idea of a television fan seem strange' (cited in Jenkins 1992: 55). He goes even further and argues that 'Viewers rarely make plans to watch TV . . . Its taken-for-grantedness makes it appear trivial, an unimportant moment in our lives, one in which we certainly invest no great energy' (Grossberg cited in Jenkins 1992: 55). And yet many years later in 1992, Grossberg develops his use of affect to consider the way fans invest themselves in their favourite texts. He argues that it '[i]s in their affective lives that fans constantly struggle to care about something, and to find the energy to survive, to find the passion necessary to imagine and enact their own projects and possibilities' (1992a: 59). He uses the term 'mattering maps' to explain the different ways in which people invest their energies and passions towards particular texts (1992: 57–8).[5] Viewers often have various programmes they have invested their energy in (in terms of watching the series) but also different levels of engagement: they might be casual fans of one programme but dedicated fans of another. Very often fans will have more than one programme they are attached to. These attachments demonstrate an emotional engagement with television and an active audience and yet most fandom is still looked upon with suspicion and derision for the reasons Jenkins outlined more than two decades ago.

Hills argues that: 'Without the emotional attachments and passions of fans, fan cultures would not exist, but fans and academics often take these attachments for granted or do not place them centre-stage in their explorations of fandom' (2002: 90). Indeed, as this chapter has explored, one of the primary reasons for the engagement fans have with particular texts is the emotional investment they make.

Grossberg's work not only illustrates a sea change in the way fandom is discussed but also, and more importantly for this work, his return to fan's affective relationship with television emphasises the importance of understanding the way viewers emotionally engage with what they watch. As this chapter has argued, fans are no longer the only viewers who binge on television series and enjoy an affective relationship with what they watch on television. Indeed, revisiting the literature on the everyday and fandom reminds us of the way in which the two areas of study are interrelated (as Livingstone has suggested before) but also underlines the way in which fandom has changed because viewers' everyday relationship to texts has altered. The introduction of DVD box sets, digital recording devices and texts that respond more directly to viewer involvement have meant that there is a different kind of emotional attachment to be explored. We might also consider that the viewing figures that once made 'serious drama' (Caughie 2000) something people would talk about and engage with have dropped dramatically. People are more likely to watch 'quality' television on DVD, often two or three episodes at a time. They are also more liable to talk about a series on the internet than over the 'watercooler'. Not only has this changed the way we think of fandom and fan cultures but also it changes the way we think about a viewer's emotional investment in television and the meanings she or he might make. Instead of dismissing those who develop an emotional engagement with what they watch as 'fans' and seeing them therefore as 'mindless' and 'uncritical', new research and viewing practices suggest that these viewers can be both emotionally close to a text *and* critical of it.

Notes

1. See Jenkins 1992: 3, 24–7.
2. Thanks to Noelani Peace for reminding me of this scene.
3. See also Jenkins 2006: 13–15.
4. See Jenkins 'sitting too close?', in *Textual Poachers* (1992).
5. Grossberg uses the term 'mattering maps' in 'The indifference of television' but in terms of the contradiction between 'ideological maps' and 'mattering maps' (1997: 142).

Questions

1. How would you define a fan? How are fans different from other viewers?
2. Discuss the ways in which fans influence/change the text?
3. Discuss the difference between a cinematic gaze and a televisual gaze. How has new technology changed our viewing practices?
4. In their work on 'cult television' Sara Gwenllian-Jones and Roberta Pearson pose the following question: 'What distinguishes "cult" programs such as *Star Trek* and *The X Files* from other series such as *Friends*, which may attract larger audiences but do not inspire significant interpretive fan cultures?' (2004: x). Consider this question and the distinction between 'fan' and 'cult' texts.

Further reading

Bausinger, Hermann (1984), 'Media, technology and daily life', *Media, Culture and Society*, 6: 343–51.

Bordwell, David (1989), *Making Meaning: Inference and Rhetoric in the Interpretation of Cinema*, Cambridge, MA: Harvard University Press.

Brooker, Will (2002), *Using the Force: Creativity, Community and Star Wars Fans*, London: Continuum.

De Certeau, Michel (1984), *The Practice of Everyday Life*, trans. Steven Rendall, Berkeley, CA: University of California Press.

Gauntlett, David, and Annette Hill (1999), *TV Living: Television, Culture and Everyday Life*, London and New York: Routledge/British Film Institute.

Gwenllian-Jones, Sara and Roberta Pearson (eds) (2004), *Cult Television*, Minneapolis: University of Minnesota Press.

Hill, Annette and Ian Calcutt, 'Vampire hunters: the scheduling and reception of *Buffy the Vampire Slayer* and *Angel* in the UK', *Intensities*, Issue 1, http://intensities.org/Essays/Hill-Calcutt.pdf.

Hills, Matt (2002), *Fan Cultures*, London and New York: Routledge.

Jenkins, Henry (1992), *Textual Poachers: Television Fans and Participatory Culture*, New York and London: Routledge.

Jenkins, Henry (2001), '*Intensities* interviews with Henry Jenkins and Matt Hills at the Console-ing Passions Conference, University of Bristol, July 7th, 2001', http://intensities.org, Issue 2.

Jenkins, Henry (2006), *Fans, Bloggers and Gamers: Exploring Participatory Culture*, New York: New York University Press.

Kompare, Derek (2006), 'Publishing flow: DVD box sets and the reconception of television', *Television & New Media*, 7(4): 335–60.

Lewis, Lisa A. (ed.) (1992), *The Adoring Audience: Fan Culture and Popular Media*, London and New York: Routledge.

Livingstone, Sonia ([1990] 1998), *Making Sense of Television: The Psychology of Audience Interpretation*, 2nd edn, New York and London: Routledge.

Philo, Greg (1999a), 'Conclusions on Media Audiences and Message Reception', in Greg Philo (ed.), *Message Received*, Harlow: Longman, pp. 282–8.

Further viewing

(Films and television series portraying fan cultures)
Galaxy Quest (Parisot 1999).
Misery (Reiner 1990).
Spaced (Channel 4 2006).
(Documentaries about fan cultures)
Fans and Freaks: The Culture of Comics and Conventions (Lackey 2002).
My Life with Count Dracula (Black 2003).
Trekkies (Nygard 1997).

3 Global Meanings and Trans-cultural Understandings of *Dallas*

> Television is not just what appears on screen; it is a variety of invisible yet specific practices that occur in the air, in orbit and across lands.
>
> (Parks 2005: 69)

The last chapter considered how television functions in the everyday or personal domain – how we feel guilty for watching too much TV, and yet keep watching it – how we sometimes have it in the background, what Gauntlett and Hill refer to as 'electronic wallpaper' (1999: 112) – how at other times it is seen as a friend or source of companionship. The last chapter also examined the ways in which this personalised medium is changing; how it is increasingly found in the public sphere and how viewers are viewing 'irrationally' with the invention of hand-held televisions, which invites questions regarding how these personalised TVs will help to further negotiate the individualised meanings we take from the screen.

We are in what has been referred to as 'TV3', which covers the period post-1995. As Nelson argues, TV3 'marks a new era hailing the triumph of digital-satellite capacity to distribute transnationally, bypassing national distribution and, in some instances, regulatory controls' (2007: 8; see also Creeber and Hills 2007). This leads to questions, rehearsed before, about how one culture is received and understood in another. It also raises questions about how advanced capitalism affects viewing. As Nelson points out, '[i]n Western culture, the increasing affluence of consumer individualism has, for good or ill, promoted immediate over deferred gratifications and the pleasures of excess' (2007: 168–9). This chapter will consider how the mediation of meaning occurs on a global scale. More specifically, it will consider how the global exchange of televisual texts affects citizenship, notions of individualism and choice and the concept of emotion.

Chapter 1 outlined the shift towards empirical and ethnographic work – one of the impacts this had was on global understandings of TV viewing. There was an assumption that the media was all-powerful and that other cultures were being imperialised, dominated by Western media, in particular by American imports. If we look at the early trade import/export of TV programmes then we might appreciate why researchers feared that other cultures were at risk. However, when scholars visited these countries they found a very different situation than the one they imagined. As Michael Tracey wrote in his seminal article, 'The poisoned chalice?': 'very general picture of TV flows . . . is not a one-way street; rather there are a number of main thorough-fares, with a series of not unimportant smaller roads' (1988: 23). Indeed, ethnographic research done by Ien Ang (1985), and Liebes and Katz (1990) in particular, illustrated that other cultures were not overly consuming Western TV, in fact in some cases it was very unpopular.

In the cases where viewers were watching American television – and *Dallas* has been the most significant case study – what researchers found is that other cultures 'read' the show in very different ways to American audiences. To use de Certeau's term, outlined in Chapter 2, other cultures had 'poached' these texts and made sense of them using their own cultural frameworks. In this way the preferred meanings, or dominant meanings were not taken on fully but mediated, opposed and sometimes resisted by alternative audiences.

In their influential collection titled *New Patterns of Global Television: Peripheral Vision*, editors John Sinclair, Elizabeth Jacka and Stuart Cunningham argue that a 'sea change' in television systems started in the late 1970s (1996: 1). These changes were part of broader move-ments happening in the Western world including: 'globalisation, trade liberalization, increased national and international competition and a decrease in the centrality of the state as a provider of goods and serv-ices' (1996: 1). New changes in technology, specifically the satellite, also meant more channels and choice in television programming. As Sinclair, Jacka and Cunningham suggest, the 'satellite has acted as a kind of "Trojan-horse" of media liberalization' (1996: 2). Until the late 1970s, North America, Latin American and Australia were the only three regions to have a mixed system of broadcasting, which is a com-bination of public and private programming (1996: 2). The change from public to private broadcasting systems meant that there was a heavy dependence on American imports (hence the popularity and world-wide distribution of *Dallas*). But it also led to more cross-cultural swaps – so the Latin American telenovellas (like soap operas) became popular in southern Europe (1996: 3) – and at the time of writing we have *Ugly Betty* (ABC 2006–) which is a telenovella popu-larised as an American TV programme. Sinclair, Jacka and Cunningham advance the idea of 'geolinguistic regions', which they describe as the 'broad proposition that export markets will develop amongst countries which share a similar language and culture' (1996: 26). Instead of thinking about the way television flows from one country to another, 'geolinguistic regions' encourages us to think about the way television is distributed to similar speaking cultures – such as the flow of the telenovella form from South America to Spain.

Cultural imperialism; media imperialism and *Dallas*

In general terms, media imperialism involves thinking that the major world source for media outputs can be found primarily in the US and secondarily in Europe, specifically the UK, and that these centres act as hubs through which all cultural products must flow (Sinclair et al. 1996: 6). In his assessment of 'Media imperialism' in the early 1980s, Fred Fejes argued that: 'A third concern that the media imperialism approach must address if it is to progress is the issue of culture' (1981: 287). As Fejes pointed out, it is necessary for researchers of media imperialism to think about the ways it affects culture. The term cultural imperialism therefore refers to the ways in which culture (language, modes of address, lifestyle, et al.) is affected by media texts. In his influential *Mass Communications and American Empire* (1969), Herbert Schiller argued that:

> The structure, character and direction of the domestic communications apparatus are no longer, if they ever were, entirely national concerns. This powerful mechanism now directly impinges on peoples' lives everywhere. It is essential therefore, that there should be at least some familiarity with what the American communications system is like, how it has evolved, what motivates it and where it is pointing. (1969: 17)

Schiller's work was among the first to look directly at the domestic and international mass communications structure and policy in the US and consider its global influence, and the influence of his work continues to dominate. Sinclair, Jacka and Cunningham refer to Schiller's work as the 'locus classicus of the cultural imperialism thesis' (1996: 6) and Jonathan Bignell and Elke Weissman suggest, 'most work takes Schiller as its starting point' (2008: 93). Indeed, recent work on global television suggests, 'there are signs of a critical reassessment of "globalisation" in favour of a more "retro" theoretical position that uses the imperialist perspective with some new insights' (Corcoran 2007: 84).

As outlined earlier, the idea that other cultures were dominated by American cultural products started to prove untrue. Theoretical perspectives such as postmodernism and postcolonialism and research into 'active' audiences caused TV theorists to reconsider this 'one-way street' model. What they found was that although there were a lot of US imports there were also local programmes that commanded large audiences. The assumption that the Western model would be more powerful overlooked alternative models that were in many cases preferred.

In *The Making of Exile Cultures: Iranian Television in Los Angeles* (1993), for instance, Hamid Naficy relates a moving anecdote about his daughter, Shayda, and his niece, Setareh, who met each other in Los Angeles and bonded over *The Little Mermaid*. Although Setareh spoke only German and Persian and Shayda could only speak English, they communicated through the songs of the popular Disney film. This experience leads him to argue that:

> The globalisation of American pop culture does not automatically translate into globalisation of American control. This globalised culture provides a shared discursive space where transnationals such as Setareh and Shayda can localise it, make their own uses of it, domesticate and indigenize it. They may think with American cultural products but they do not think American. (Naficy 1993: 2)

Naficy's point is important insofar as it challenges the suggestion that American products will turn their consumers into Americans. His work also continues the idea that viewers and consumers communicate through products, they are not dominated by them. His experience also provides us with an emotional account of how film and television provides a platform through which people can communicate. The songs allowed Seterah and Shayda to feel a sense of connection, despite the differences in their background and language.

Ien Ang begins her study of the world's most watched television programme by pointing out that the early 1980s marked a 'new, spectacular phenomenon: *Dallas*'. 'This unique status', Ang tells us, 'is due first and foremost to the extraordinary but undeniable popularity achieved by this American dramatic serial about a rich Texan oil family . . . No other fictional programme, foreign or domestic, has ever achieved such high viewing figures' (1985: 1). *Dallas* sparked a host of academic studies and articles; one of the best known of these is Tamar Liebes and Elihu Katz's study of the reception of Dallas in 1990, which they titled *The Export of Meaning*. It is a study of audience reactions on three continents. Liebes and Katz pose the following questions: 'How in the world is a programme like Dallas so universally understandable, or is it? Is it understood in the same way in different places? Does it evoke different kinds of involvement and response?' (1990: 3). Liebes and Katz use their study of *Dallas* to make broader assertions about TV, its role in identity construction, its role in terms of nationality, the way we watch TV and the way we make meanings from it – and how this *export of meaning* functions. They begin with a discussion of 'cultural imperialism' but argue that labelling something imperialistic is not the same thing as proving it; they argue that in order to prove a TV show is imperialistic you demonstrate the following:

> (1) that there is a message incorporated in the program that is designed to profit American interests overseas, (2) that the message is decoded by the receiver in the way it was encoded by the sender, (3) that it is accepted uncritically by the viewers and allowed to seep into their culture. (1990: 4)

They also propose three reasons for the worldwide success of American television:

> (1) the universality, or primordiality, of some of its themes and formulae, which makes programmes psychologically accessible; (2) the polyvalent or open potential of many of the stories, and thus their value as projective mechanisms and as material for negotiation and play in the families of man; and (3) the sheer availability of American programmes in a marketplace where national producers – however zealous – cannot fill more than a fraction of the hours they feel they must provide. (1990: 5)

Why *Dallas*? Ang counted ninety countries in which *Dallas* succeeded. In fact it only failed in a few places: Brazil and Japan in particular (see Liebes and Katz 1990: Chapter 9). As a result *Dallas* became one of the most studied texts in the history of television research. However, Sinclair, Jacka and Cunningham argue that the 'export of meaning' is not 'just a matter of viewer reception' (1996: 184). Many nations, they argue, place special importance on the international profile they can establish with their audiovisual exports. They use the example of Australia and *Neighbours*. What they ask us to do is to consider the importance of 'regional' identities as much as global ones. Part of Sinclair, Jacka and Cunningham's project is to argue that the cultural imperialism thesis implies a 'dichotomised view of "the West" versus the "Third world"' and leaves out 'semi-peripheral settler societies such as Australia and Canada' (1996: 9). They argue that: 'Within the Anglophone world, Australia and Canada, and even the UK, produce programmes which have assimilated the genre conventions of US television, but with their own look and feel' (1996: 13). Jonathan Bignell and Elke Weissman's Arts and Humanities Research Council (AHRC) research project 'British Television and Acquired US Programmes, 1970–2000' has tried to redress this as has recent work such as Paul Rixon's *American Television on British Screens: A Story of Cultural Interaction* (2006) and Jeffrey Miller's *Something Completely Different: British Television and American Culture* (2000).

Lisa Parks's work on satellites in *Cultures in Orbit: Satellites and the Televisual* (2005) provides us with another example, not only on the way exports are read in other cultures but also of how *Dallas* is understood in the 'outback'. Focusing on the ways in which satellites are used and how this use tells us something about cultural practice allows Parks to comment both on the indigenous culture she visits and the global presence it mediates. She argues that:

> Aboriginal Australians who own and operate Imparja TV use satellites not just to downlink, dub, and rerun American and British programs and flow structures; rather, they select shows and arrange them in ways that give shape and meaning to the Imparja footprint . . . Imparja's flow can be conceived as hybrid in the sense that it represents a rewriting or reconfiguration of television programming made for audiences elsewhere. (2005: 63)

Similar to the research discussed in Liebes and Katz's *Export of Meaning*, Parks witnesses the way in which Indigenous Australians make meaning out of the television exports instead of having meaning forced upon them. Her research leads her to suggest that we imagine 'flow' and 'footprint' 'not as fixed schedules and closed boundaries but as zones of situated knowledges and cultural incongruities that may compel struggles for cultural survival rather than simply suppress them' (2005: 62). In imagining more permeable and moveable boundaries, Parks's work supports the notion of an active audience and continues a line of research that interrogates the notion of cultural imperialism.

The research discussed so far places emphasis on nationality in its discussion of spatial flows. Borders are used to make suggestions about the ways in which meanings and identities are organised. Michael Curtin suggests rethinking the idea of nationality to consider instead the ways in which 'media capitals' affect flow. Curtin defines 'media capitals' as a 'nexus or switching point, rather than a container'; they are 'particular cities that have become centres for the finance, production and distribution of television programs; cities like Bombay, Cairo and Hong Kong' (2003: 203). Instead of thinking about the ways in which nations affect content (through regulatory constraints), Curtin's research suggests that particular cities across the globe are responsible for the production and distribution of television content. He argues that 'neo-network' television firms now focus their attention on marketing and promotion, which marks a change from the network era where the control of a handful of national channels was the 'key to profitability' (2003: 212). According to Curtin, this means that certain series, such as *Star Trek*, or production companies, such as Disney animation, become dominant global brands: '[g]iven a greater range of choices, audiences are drawn to products by textual elements – characters, storylines, special effects – rather than by the technological and regulatory constraints formerly imposed on the delivery system' (Curtin 2003: 212). Unlike previous models of global television, which focus on the ways in which nations affect the cultural output on television through regulations and policy, Curtin's work suggests that textual elements carry a significant weight when it comes to why people watch certain programmes.

Cultural citizenship, convergence and emotion

We are in a crisis of belonging, a population crisis, of who, what, when, and where. More and more people feel as though they *do not* belong. More and more people are *seeking* to belong, and more and more people are not *counted* as belonging.

So begins Toby Miller's book titled *Cultural Citizenship: Cosmopolitanism, Consumerism and Television in a Neoliberal Age* (2007: 1, author's italics). Miller's pronouncement regarding the state of the world and its citizens urge us to think more radically about the ways in which belonging becomes a very important issue in contemporary society. I would argue that part of this desire to belong can not only be found expressed through fictional and factual storylines on television but also in the way people get emotionally involved with what they watch.

In his work on 'convergence culture', Henry Jenkins defines convergence as 'the flow of content across multiple media platforms, the cooperation between multiple media industries, and the migratory behaviour of media audiences who will go almost anywhere in search of the kinds of entertainment experiences they want' (2006: 2). In other words, Jenkins is not just thinking about the technological development of media forms and the ways in which they affect each other – he is also thinking about the ways in which technological developments affect culture and affect people's use of media in their everyday lives. Convergence in Jenkins's work is not just about television being like the internet and the internet like television, but also the way in which people will seek information and new ways of connection through various media platforms (2006: 3).

Jenkins's interpretation of convergence leads him to come up with the term, 'affective economics'. He argues that 'according to the logic of "affective economics," the ideal consumer is active, emotionally engaged, and socially networked' (2006: 20). One example of the kind of convergence and 'affective economics' that Jenkins refers to can be found on the websites of television programmes such as *Lost* and *24*. On these websites users can download 'mobisodes' at a cost to see some extra scenes not aired on television. Users can also play themed games and be sent on a 'Jack Bauer'-esque mission through their mobile phones. Here technologies converge: television, the internet and mobiles work together to provide a service to their user. But, as Jenkins suggests, this is also about 'affective economics' as the websites rely on the fact that their viewers will be emotionally involved enough in the series to want to pay to find out more about the show or to experience simulated stories related to the programmes they enjoy.

Recent sociological literature on the concept of individualism, including primarily the work of Anthony Giddens (1990, 1991), Ulrich Beck and Elisabeth Beck-Gernsheim (2001) and Zygmunt Bauman (2001), illustrates the demand on the individual to be self-reflexive and to self-monitor and yet to be aware of the risks posed by modern society. Beck, for instance, suggests that

> individualisation is a compulsion, albeit a paradoxical one, to create, to stage manage, not only one's own biography but the bonds and networks surrounding it and to do this amid changing preferences and at successive stages of life, while constantly adapting to the conditions of the labour market, the education system, the welfare state and so on. (2001: 4)

Following the work of these authors, it is clear that we have moved into a culture that values and reiterates the position and privilege of the individual.

This culture of individualism has given way to what Elliott and Lemert refer to as 'privatised worlds'. In *The New Individualism: The Emotional Costs of Globalization* (2006) Elliott and Lemert chart a shift from a politicised culture to a privatised culture. Drawing on work by Beck, among others, they consider the impact of 'reflexive individualism' and the way in which it places emphasis on 'choosing, changing and transforming' (Elliott and Lemert 2006: 97). They also consider how the emphasis on the individual and private worlds has led to a 'confessional therapeutic culture', found in TV talk shows such as *The Oprah Winfrey Show*, and, increasingly, as I shall go on to argue in Chapter 7, in reality and lifestyle programming.

The shift to a more individualised society and emphasis on 'choice' impacts on not just *what* we watch but *how* we watch it. In terms of programming, as discussed in the last chapter, the emphasis on consumerism is evident in the television 'tie-ins' and websites that cater to an individual interaction with the programme and its characters. Recording devices such as TiVo mean that viewers can choose what they watch and when they want to watch it. Interactive devices (such as the 'red button') put the viewer in control of what they watch.

This sense of choice, control and interactivity has led some scholars to think that fans/viewers have more power over what they watch than ever before. In his research on audiences and TV3, discussed briefly in the last chapter, Derek Johnson cites examples in which fans or avid watchers of series are invited by the producers to write episodes, both in an effort to involve the audience but also within a strategy to acquire 'free labour' (2007: 69). However, Johnson is wary of the true welcome producers give these fan writers and argues that 'production institutions simultaneously work to manage fan proximities and bring them under industrial control' (2007: 84). In 'inviting' fans and avid watchers in, producers both benefit from the 'free labour' of their knowledge and maintain control over their participation. So while fans are more involved than before, they are also under more control.

It is important to note that convergence does not just affect what we watch but it also affects the way we negotiate personal relationships. Jenkins reminds us that

> Convergence doesn't just involve commercially produced materials and services travelling along well regulated and predictable circuits . . . Our lives, relationships, memories, fantasies, desires also flow across media channels. Being a lover or a mommy or a teacher occurs on multiple platforms. (2007: 17)

Indeed, many of us rely on our mobile phones, email or web cameras to communicate intimacy and emotion to those who are both near and far. As someone who lives in the UK but whose family is mostly in the US, I have had to become comfortable with expressing my feelings through media channels and not through face-to-face contact. This has become a reality for many and reminds us of the ways in which our emotions are often mediated through various impersonal forms. The next two chapters will focus on the ways in which the concepts of emotion and affect are theorised, particularly within feminist and film theory.

Exercises

1. How would you define 'media convergence'? How do you think new technologies will influence/change viewer's engagements with television?
2. Read Liebes and Katz's chapter entitled 'One Moroccan Group: A Transcript and Commentary' (1990: 34–67). Pay careful attention to the way they annotate the transcript, drawing on audience research models (discussed in Chapter 1). Design a research outline (see also ibid.: Chapter 3) for your own transnational television research project.
3. How might an emphasis on 'choice' affect television programming?

Further reading

Ang, Ien (1985), *Watching Dallas: Soap Opera and the Melodramatic Imagination*, London and New York: Routledge.

Barker, Chris (1997), *Global Television: An Introduction*, Malden, MA: Blackwell.

Bignell, Jonathan and Elke Weissman (2008), 'Cultural difference? Not so different after all', *Critical Studies in Television* 3(1) Spring: 93–8.

Curran, James and Myung-Jin Park (eds) (2000), *De-Westernizing Media Studies*, London: Routledge.

Curtin, Michael (2003), 'Media Capital: Towards the Study of Spatial Flows', *International Journal of Cultural Studies*, 6(2): 202–28.

Fejes, Fred (1981), 'Media imperialism: an assessment', *Media, Culture & Society*, 3: 281–9.

Liebes, Tamar and Elihu Katz (1990) *The Export of Meaning: Cross-Cultural Readings of Dallas*, New York and Oxford: Oxford University Press.

Lull, James (ed.) (1988), *World Families Watch Television*, London: Sage.

Lull, James (2007), 'Television and communicational space: the clash of global hegemonies', *New Review of Film and Television Studies*, 5(1): 97–110.

Miller, Toby (2007), *Cultural Citizenship: Cosmopolitanism, Consumerism and Television in a Neoliberal Age*, Philadelphia: Temple University Press.

Naficy, Hamid (1993), *The Making of Exile Cultures: Iranian Television in Los Angeles*, Minneapolis: University of Minnesota Press.

Parks, Lisa (2005), *Cultures in Orbit: Satellites and the Televisual*, Durham, NC: Duke University Press.

Pratt, Mary Louise ([1992] 2008), *Imperial Eyes: Travel Writing and Transculturation*, 2nd edn, London and New York: Routledge.

Sinclair, J., E. Jacka and S. Cunningham (1996), *Peripheral Vision: New Patterns in Global Television*, Oxford: Oxford University Press.

Tracey, Michael (1985), 'The poisoned chalice? International television and the idea of dominance', *Daedalus*, 114(4): 17–56.

4 Theorising Emotion and Affect: feminist engagements

There is a long history of theoretical work on emotion and affect. Indeed Ann Cvetkovich argues that 'the representation of social problems as affective dilemmas can be traced to its origins in eighteenth- and nineteenth-century culture' (1992: 2). More recently, in the 1980s, feminist theorists such as Lila Abu-Lughod (1986), Arlie Russell Hochschild (1985), bell hooks (1989), Alison Jaggar (1989), Audre Lorde (1984), Elizabeth Spelman (1989) and Catherine Lutz (1988) took interest in women's emotional lives and labours.[1] While these earlier influences are still resonant, it is only over the last decade that we have witnessed what Woodward (1996), Berlant (1997) and Nicholson (1999) have referred to as an 'affective turn'. Interestingly, this turn is not specific to cultural studies; it extends into the field of neurology, where writers such as Antonio Damasio (1994, 2003) have reconsidered the connection between emotion and rationality. Other work on emotion and affect, such as Robert Solomon's *In Defense of Sentimentality* (2004) and *The Passions: Emotion and the Meaning of Life* (1993), Jack Katz's *How Emotions Work* (1999), Martha Nussbaum's *Upheavals of Thought* (2001), Jenefer Robinson's *Deeper Than Reason* (2005), David Eng and David Kazanjian's *On Loss* (2003), Brian Massumi's *Parables for the Virtual: Movement, Affect, Sensation* (2002), Rei Terada's *Feeling in Theory: Emotion after the "Death of the Subject"* (2001), Anthony Elliott and Charles Lemert's *The New Individualism: The Emotional Costs of Globalisation* (2006), to name but a few,[2] illustrate the renewed and continuing interest in this field and its significance within critical theory.

The authors discussed in this chapter continue the interest in the emotional lives and labours of women that feminist theorists addressed in the 1980s but concentrate more specifically on a theoretical framework for emotion and affect with a view to deepening our understanding of these concepts. In attempting to address so many books in a short chapter I am aware that I cannot do justice to the rich terrain each offer. Instead I shall map out some concerns that seem to be important across the genre: the place of emotion in the public sphere; the way in which this intrusion of emotion has refigured the feminist mantra 'the personal is the political'; and the debate on how feelings work towards social good. While this chapter will focus primarily on theorising the concepts of emotion and affect within feminist theory, the final section turns to work that bridges the gap between theorising emotion and studying it in relation to television and ethnography.

Emotion vs. affect

The nature and degree of difference between emotion and affect is often contested. Some argue that emotion refers to a sociological expression of feelings whereas affect is more firmly rooted in biology and in our physical response to feelings; others attempt to differentiate on the basis that emotion requires a subject while affect does not;[3] and some ignore these distinctions altogether. Elspeth Probyn, for instance, suggests that: 'A basic distinction is that emotion refers to cultural and social expression, whereas affects are of a biological and physiological nature' (2005: 11). By contrast, Sianne Ngai, in her work on 'ugly feelings', argues that:

> At the end of the day, the difference between emotion and affect is still intended to solve the same basic and fundamentally descriptive problem it was coined in psychoanalytic practice to solve: that of distinguishing first-person from third-person feeling, and, by extension, feeling that is contained by an identity from feeling that is not. (2005: 27)

For these reasons as well as others, Ngai uses emotion and affect interchangeably. Titles such as Teresa Brennan's *Transmission of Affect* (2004) and Sara Ahmed's *The Cultural Politics of Emotion* (2004) may gesture towards an emphasis each author places on either emotion or affect: however, this rarely means that only one or the other is explored. Indeed, all of the works discussed in this chapter place importance on the way in which feeling is negotiated in the public sphere and experienced through the body.

While each author appropriates an impressive range of material in their examination of emotion and/or affect, including insights from writers as diverse as Sigmund Freud, Karl Marx, Michel Foucault, Charles Darwin, J. L. Austin, Raymond Williams and Judith Butler, most also include work on affect by American psychologist Silvan Tomkins. Tomkins's work has gained significance in the last decade or so, particularly after the publication of *Shame and Its Sisters: A Silvan*

Tomkins Reader (1995), edited by Eve Kosofsky Sedgwick and Adam Frank. He has been compared to Freud as a 'figure through whose work a lot of sharply different, competing, and often conflicting interpretive paths require to be cleared' (Tomkins 1995: 24). In his work, Tomkins designates affects as a primary motivational system and considers shame, interest, surprise, joy, anger, fear, distress and disgust as the basic set of affects (Tomkins 1995: 5). However, he distinguishes shame and disgust from the others as affects that construct a 'boundary line or barrier' (Tomkins 1995: 22).

In their introduction to Tomkins's work, Eve Sedgwick and Adam Frank argue that Tomkins's theory on affect works to defend against teleological presumptions that are rooted in the disciplines of psychology. In other words, Tomkins does not offer a causal side to affect as is evident in statements such as: 'It is enjoyable to enjoy. It is exciting to be excited' (Tomkins 1995: 7). Unlike Freud's work, where to enjoy means one thing and to be excited means something else – and both have something to do with heterosexual sexuality and its repression – Tomkins's understanding of affect 'is indifferent to the means-end difference' (Tomkins 1995: 7). For Sedgwick and Frank this means, among other things, that Tomkins's work on affect poses a resistance to heterosexist teleologies; not so much because his is an anti-homophobic project but, rather, because he finds 'a different place to begin' (1995: 7).

The personal is the political

In the preface to *Mixed Feelings: Feminism, Mass Culture and Victorian Sentimentalism* (1992), Ann Cvetkovich explains that the movement towards the personal within feminist theory meant that the personal and its healing became the solution to problems that were largely collective and social: women began to tell individual stories in order to heal themselves while overlooking the fact that other women were suffering in similar ways. As she argues: 'If nineteenth-century culture *constructed* the distinction between the personal and the political, then the contemporary claim that the personal is political does not mean that the personal as it currently exists is political' (1992: 3). One of the central concerns in work on emotion and affect is the intrusion of the private into the public sphere, what Lauren Berlant refers to as the 'intimate public sphere' (1997: 4). In *The Queen of America Goes to Washington City*, Berlant argues that:

> The transgressive logic of the feminist maxim 'The personal is the political,' which aimed radically to make the affects and acts of

intimacy in everyday life the index of national/sexual politics and ethics, has now been reversed and redeployed on behalf of a staged crisis in the legitimacy of the most traditional, apolitical, sentimental patriarchal family values. Today, the primary guiding maxim might be, 'The political is the personal'. (1997: 177–8)

This reversal of 'the personal is the political' to 'the political is the personal', as Berlant suggests, means that something intimate, such as sex, is being used, not as a means to reveal unethical power, but instead to suggest that 'abnormal' sexual practices illustrate a threat against the nation (and therefore the need for good old 'family' values) (1997: 178). Using what she refers to as a 'counterpolitics of the silly object', Berlant interrogates the 'waste materials of everyday communication' (1997: 12) to examine the ways in which intimacy figures national culture. Through a reading of texts such as *The Simpsons*, *Forrest Gump* and *Once Around* she considers issues regarding 'pregnancy/citizenship' (the American abortion debate); 'diva citizenship' and the 'face of America'. In so doing, her book offers a fundamental critique of the right-wing agenda in America and a crucial insight into the use of intimacy in the public sphere.

In *Intimacy* (2000), a collection of essays on the relationship between the intimate and the public, Berlant goes on to argue that: 'the inwardness of the intimate is met by a corresponding publicness . . . At present, in the U.S., therapy saturates the scene of intimacy, from psychoanalysis and twelve-step groups to girl talk, talk shows, and other witnessing genres' (2000: 1). The essays in this collection, some of which were first published in an award-winning issue of *Critical Inquiry*, seek to address the 'contradictory desires' that 'mark the intimacy of daily life' (2000: 5). Berlant's work, in particular, has been addressed recently by theorists who find her explication of the way in which the intimate meets the public useful in articulating the relationship between emotion and the public sphere.

Cvetkovich's work, for example, 'explor[es] affective life as an index of public cultures and social systems' (2003: 285).[4] Her book is organised as an 'archive of feelings' and by this Cvetkovich means that she seeks to explore cultural texts as repositories of feelings and emotions that are bound not only by their content but by their production (2003: 7). One of the aims of her work is to consider how affect, and in particular the affects associated with trauma, function as a foundation for the formation of public cultures (2003: 10). However, Cvetkovich takes the 'nation as a space of struggle' (2003: 16) as a departure point in order to uncover traumas that have been overlooked or marginalised. She does not look toward the Hollywood blockbuster or spectacular media events – she 'resists the way that trauma can be used to reinforce nationalism when constructed as a wound that must be healed in the name of unity' (2003: 16).

So, for example, Cvetkovich focuses on more localised and marginalised work, such as Lisa Kron's *2.5 Minute Ride* and sees it as 'a reflection of [her] use of both a minoritizing approach, exploring the specificity of lesbian texts, and a universalizing one, emphasizing their continuities with other texts of trauma' (2003: 29). However, in the epilogue Cvetkovich makes reference to Kimberly Pierce's *Boys Don't Cry* (1999) in which she considers 'whose feelings count' in relation to the Teena Brandon story. She states that:

> In aiming to make lesbian feelings and the publics they construct visible, I am emphatically not trying to make them equivalent to the public spheres that have been constructed around historical traumas such as the Holocaust or slavery. My argument is not based on a model of inclusion in which lesbian cultures get equal time alongside other groups. (2003, 279)

These two examples, which stand at either end of her work, expose some of the tensions and contradictions that are inherent in her project. That is, they reflect a tendency on Cvetkovich's part to use lesbian public cultures as private instances of public trauma, and yet, at the same time, she resists allowing them to stand equally alongside other instances of public mourning.

One of the directions in which the interest in the divide between the personal and political takes us is towards a consideration of public displays of sentimentalism. In her chapter entitled 'Some WHYS and *why mes?*' Denise Riley refers to the handwritten cards, flowers and teddy bears that grace scenes of public mourning. The cards contain the question Why? And, as Riley argues: 'Such cards have become part of today's panoply of public mourning.' These public demonstrations of mourning lead Riley to consider how

> this WHY, a prostrated inert thing, is also a provocation. To whom is it put? The writers of such cards will realize perfectly well that the only answer to their implied "Why was this innocent life destroyed?" is swift and brutal-sounding: that here there is no *why* to be answered other than by a terse *because*. (2005: 59)

Her analysis of these public displays also leads her to consider why these metaphysical interrogatives have replaced questions of moral responsibility, such as: "'I must be involved in this somewhere" vying with "I am not responsible for this"' (2005: 69). Perhaps we can turn here to earlier work by Berlant in which she suggests that 'public sentimentality is too often a defensive response by people who identify with privilege, yet fear they will be exposed as immoral by their tacit sanction of a particular structural violence that benefits them' (2000b: 33). 'Why?' and 'why me?' allow the speaker to replace moral responsibility with destiny and bad fortune. One might also think of the way in which people refer to an event as 'tragic' instead of attending to the political or social structures that allow these 'tragic' events to happen. Interest in the intimate and affective responses of the public emphasise the need to clarify the use of the feminist mantra 'the personal is the political' in order that individual stories do not replace social struggle and intimacy is not used to legitimise patriarchal family values.

Models of affective contagion

Anna Gibbs opens her discussion on 'contagious feelings' with the following:

> Bodies can catch feelings as easily as catch fire: affect leaps from one body to another, evoking tenderness, inciting shame, igniting rage, exciting fear – in short, communicable affect can inflame nerves and muscles in a conflagration of every conceivable kind of passion. (2001)

Gibbs's description of the 'catchy' way in which feelings affect the body gesture toward a model of affective contagion that is offered in work by Teresa Brennan and Sara Ahmed. Brennan, for instance, begins her exploration of affect with the following question: 'Is there anyone who has not, at least once, walked into a room and "felt the atmosphere?"' (2004: 1). She argues that an increase in the perceived 'catchiness' of emotions 'makes the Western individual especially more concerned with securing a private fortress, personal boundaries, against the unsolicited emotional intrusions of the other' (ibid.: 15).

Brennan draws on biochemistry and neurology in her assessment of affect. For instance, she refers to the neurological term 'entrainment', which is the process 'whereby one person's or one group's nervous and hormonal systems are brought into alignment with another's' (ibid.: 9). An example of chemical entrainment, for instance, is pheromones – molecules that communicate chemical information, which Brennan suggests, are crucial in how we 'feel the atmosphere' or how we pick up on another's mood (ibid.: 9). Her work, therefore, pays close attention to both the cultural and biological factors that contribute to the transmission of affect. Avoiding a distinction between the biological and the psychosocial, and perhaps influenced by her earlier work on hysteria,[5] Brennan's work is complimented by other projects, such as Elizabeth A. Wilson's *Psychosomatic: Feminism and the Neurological Body* (2004), which encourage feminism to embrace neurological accounts of the emotions in that they may offer a more grounded approach to feminist theories of affectivity and embodiment (Wilson 2004: 83).

According to Brennan, as people fear the emotional intrusions of the other, they begin to retreat and fortify their own surroundings. It might reasonably be argued that one aspect of this process is the rise of DIY (do-it-yourself) and lifestyle television programmes that help foster a tendency towards people creating their own sense of home. She argues that:

> The transmission of affect, whether it is grief, anxiety, or anger, is social or psychological in origin. But the transmission is also respon- sible for bodily changes; some are brief changes, as in a whiff of the room's atmosphere, some longer lasting. In other words, the trans- mission of affect, if only for an instant, alters the biochemistry and neurology of the subject. The "atmosphere" or the environment literally gets into the individual. (2004: 1)

Similarly, in her work on shame, Probyn argues that '[t]elevision in particular exploits the individual viewer's response to what resembles an intimate shared shameful moment, which is aired for all to see' (2005: 85–6). Television becomes, as Probyn points out, a particular exploiter of these catchy emotions. However, as Ahmed (2004) has argued, it is important to make a distinction between thinking about catchy emotions as property, something one has and then passes on, and thinking about how the objects of emotion circulate. As Ahmed suggests: 'even when we feel we have the same feeling, we don't neces- sarily have the same relationship to the feeling' (2004: 10). Consequently, while television may construct intimate moments, as Probyn describes, this does not necessarily mean that viewers will experience emotion or *catch* emotion in the same ways – some will laugh, some cry and some will feel bored by the same moment.

In her work on the 'cultural politics of emotion', Sara Ahmed deploys a model of affective contagion, focusing more on what emotions do and how they circulate, rather than what they are.[6] As she suggests, 'emo- tions are not simply something "I" or "we" have. Rather, it is through emotions, or how we respond to objects and others, that surfaces or boundaries are made: the "I" and the "we" are shaped by, and even take the shape of, contact with others' (2004: 10). One of the emotions

Ahmed draws particular attention to in terms of contagion is 'disgust'. Drawing on Darwin's description of a 'native's' disgust at foreign food and of his own disgust at the closeness of the 'naked savage's' body to his food, Ahmed considers how this emotion circulates and racially configures bodies. She draws attention to the ambivalent structure of disgust that involves both attraction and repulsion for its objects. For this reason, proximity and distance become crucial in thinking through the affect of disgust – the closer one is to the disgusting object the more one's body will pull back in abjection. Ahmed also considers the way in which disgust 'sticks' to some objects more than others and how disgust works performatively 'not only as the intensification of contact between bodies and objects, but also as a speech act' (2004: 92).

One of the issues that these models of affective contagion raise are that of proximity and distance – how do spatial relationships affect the way we *feel*? How do these models of contagion respond to issues such as race? Ahmed refers to an '"inside out" model of emotions' (2004: 9) which underlines the way 'we respond to objects and others, that surfaces and boundaries are made: the "I" and "we" are shaped by, and even take the shape of, contact with others' (2004: 10). Ahmed draws on emotional responses to fear, specifically those that are incited by racial difference. Referring to an excerpt from Fanon's *Black Skins, White Masks* (1986), she draws attention to the way fear does not simply move from the inside of one body to the outside of its object; instead, she argues, fear works to establish a relationship between subject and object: 'Fear involves relationships of proximity, which are crucial to establishing the "apartness" of white bodies' (Ahmed 2004: 63). This model of fear allows us to consider how 'fear works to align bodily and social space' (2004: 70), which has significant implications not only in configuring issues related to ethnicity but also in terms of a feminist reading (which Ahmed also explores). Brennan's and Ahmed's work reminds us of the way in which the study of emotion is linked to an understanding of the relations of the private or personal to the public and social.

Language as affect

Language is central to all the projects discussed and most authors are interested in the performativity of language and its ability to move people into action. Denise Riley's work, in particular, recognises the way language affects our sense of self and place in the world. As Lynn Pearce argues in her review of Riley's work: 'At the heart of [Riley's] argument sits the provocative claim that the structures of everyday language are as – if not *more* – responsible for the production of our affective selves as our unconscious psyches' (2006: 365). In Riley's consideration of how racist speech works on its targets in 'malediction', for instance, she argues that the words themselves are injurious and lodge themselves inside their victim vampirically. She imagines these bad words as seeds that, upon falling on 'some kind of linguistic soil' take root in the past memories these words conjure and evoke (Riley 2005: 11). Instead of being able to shrug these words off, people often allow them to take hold and to justify their own bad feelings. In other words, our early experiences of emotion will affectively frame our reactions in later life. If someone is used to being called 'stupid', for example, then she will be more likely to accept the accusation as correct; as if in order to 'justify the decades of unhappiness that it has caused her, she almost needs the accusation to be correct – as much as in the same breath, she vehemently repudiates it' (ibid.: 15).

However, as Riley goes on to explore, the accuser does not have as much control over these malicious words as is sometimes imagined. Riley suggests that 'the more intense the anger, the less the sense of any agency its utterer possesses' (ibid.: 18). Her exploration of the positions that both the accused and the accuser take illustrates the lack of agency in *both* positions – it emphasises the way in which emotion takes over the linguistic power and concomitant affect it has on both parties.

The essays in Sedgwick's *Touching Feeling: Affect, Pedagogy, Performativity* (2003), drawing primarily on J. L. Austin's *How to Do Things with Words* (1962), the introductory volume of Foucault's *History of Sexuality* (1978), Judith Butler's *Gender Trouble* (1990), and the first three volumes of Silvan Tomkins's *Affect, Imagery, Consciousness* (1962–92) explore, as the subtitle suggests, affect, pedagogy and performativity. Although much of the work in this collection has been published previously, the project stands on its own and offers a coherent and evocative meditation on affect. In the playfully titled chapter 'Paranoid reading and reparative reading, or, you're so paranoid, you probably think this essay is about you', for example, Sedgwick argues that 'paranoia tends to be contagious; more specifically, paranoia is drawn toward and tends to construct symmetrical relations, in particular, symmetrical epistemologies' (2003: 126). The structure of paranoia is anticipatory, reflexive and mimetic. As Sedgwick explains: 'Paranoia proposes both *Anything you can do (to me) I can do worse*, and *Anything you can do (to me) I can do first* – to myself' (ibid.: 131, author's italics). For Sedgwick, 'paranoia is offered as the example par excellence of what Tomkins refers to as "strong affect theory" ("a strong humiliation-fear theory")' (ibid.: 133). Sedgwick explains that for

Tomkins there is no difference between affect theory espoused by scientists and philosophers and affect theory generated from the analysing all people do when they try to make sense of their own reactions or those of others (ibid.: 133–4). She uses the distinction Tomkins draws between 'strong' and 'weak' theory in order to suggest that critical theorists might not want to draw 'much ontological distinction between academic theory and everyday theory' (ibid.:, 145). Sedgwick also draws on this distinction and on the concept of paranoia itself to consider a lack in contemporary theoretical vocabularies of the discussion of the value of reparative reading. She argues that: 'No less acute than a paranoid position . . . the reparative reading position undertakes a different range of affects, ambitions, and risks' (ibid.: 150) and therefore it is useful, particularly, as she argues in terms of queer readings, to reconsider these practices.

Shame

Although emotions and affects as diverse as hate, paranoia, envy, and anxiety, are explored throughout these books, 'shame' stands out as a topic that most of the authors explore, particularly in relation to feminist theory. Probyn's work focuses on shame in particular, and is the only work of the ones explored here that chooses one emotion/affect in particular as a site of inquiry. In *Blush: Faces of Shame*, Elspeth Probyn draws on Tomkins's work (as well as others) to read for a positive and productive understanding of shame. She argues that

> in shame, the feeling and minding and thinking and social body comes alive. It's in this sense that shame is positive and productive, even or especially when it feels bad. The feeling of shame teaches us about our relations to others. Shame makes us feel proximity differently . . . (2005: 34–5)

For Tomkins, shame is activated by an incomplete reduction of interest or joy (Tomkins 1995: 134). In other words, when we feel shame our feelings of joy or interest are reduced, but not completely lost. He offers the example of a child who, when meeting a stranger, might peek at the person through his or her fingers. The child may feel shame but is not completely uninterested in knowing or seeing who the stranger is. In this way, shame is also an ambivalent act, similar to the way Freud describes scopophilia. As Tomkins writes: 'In shame I wish to continue to look and to be looked at, but I also do not wish to do so' (Tomkins 1995: 137). In this way, the distinction between subject and object is lost: 'In contrast to all other affects, shame is an experience of the self by the self' (Tomkins 1995: 136). In considering the reasons why shame and pride are such central motives, Tomkins believes that the answer lies in the fact that the face is more prominent in shame than in other affects. Because the eyes both receive and send messages regarding shame, the face takes on an unusually significant role and therefore shame becomes a more potent affect than others, such as terror or anger.

Shame is taken up in particular by Ahmed and Probyn as a way of considering the discourse and performance of reconciliation in Australia (see also Biddle 1997). As Ahmed argues: 'Shame becomes crucial to the process of reconciliation or the healing of past wounds' (Ahmed 2004: 101). In her examination of 'national shame' in *Bringing Them Home* (1997) and the Sorry Books, Ahmed interrogates 'the relation between the desire to feel better and the recognition of injustice' (Ahmed 2004: 102). Ahmed describes the Sorry Books as 'one aspect of the process of reconciliation, which has also included Sorry Days (2004: 110). They are a collection of messages, statements and signatures by individual Australians (mostly white, but some indigenous Australians are also included) 'which create the effect of a shared narrative of sorrow as well as an account of national shame' (Ahmed 2004: 110). In particular Ahmed analyses the movement from 'I' to 'we' that characterises these texts and calls upon witnesses to see the way in which the nation performs its shame and yet, evades any real admission of guilt or offer of retribution: '*what is shameful is passed over through the enactment of shame*' (2004: 120, author's italics). The performance of shame fails to clarify what people are shameful for – why they are enacting that shame. Instead, as Ahmed argues, what comes through in this enactment is a desire to make sure the nation is seen to be living up to its ideals. The enactment of shame therefore becomes more important, in terms of *appearing* shameful, than the reason for the shame.

In her consideration of national shame, Probyn draws on two personal experiences, a trip to Uluru, the Aboriginal name for what some still refer to as 'Ayers Rock', and a moment at the Australian Reconciliation Convention, in order to consider both the difference between guilt and shame and also the difference between individual feelings of shame and a wider politics of shame. In the first example, the trip to Uluru, Probyn recalls sobbing as she approached the site. Drawing attention to her physical reaction, Probyn reminds us of the way in which the body participates in and acts out emotion. Our feelings are not just registered in our conscious awareness but are *felt* and enacted by our bodies. Considering whether her tears are an admission of guilt or an expression of shame, Probyn draws on Bourdieu's notion of the 'habitus' to demonstrate that 'our bodies and their biographies may be more complicated than we've given them credit for' (Probyn 2005: 72). In other words, Probyn resists a neat split between 'biological affect' and 'biographical emotion' in her assessment of shame's effects.

Probyn draws on another example, a moment when she failed to follow the silent cues of those around her, to consider the embodiment of shame and the ways in which it becomes political. She recounts being at the Australian Reconciliation Convention with her girlfriend, a white woman who had more experience of political protocol than Probyn. Again, in her description of the event, Probyn refers directly to the ways in which her body physically responds to the emotional 'air' of the room. She tells her reader that she would have liked to be invisible and yet wanted to belong. Her reaction to this was to smile at the people around her. This smile, which she also refers to as a kind of 'grimace' (2005: 96) is familiar to many of us. When we feel out of place, not quite sure of our surroundings, we might smile to show our interest and yet to mask our feelings of insecurity and awkwardness. In response to John Howard's address, many of the people in the convention stood up and turned their backs to him – to physically mark their disapproval and to shame him. Caught up in the moment, Probyn failed to realise that everyone had risen and was caught sitting down. The moment leads her to consider how white shame moved from an 'I' to a 'we', similar to Ahmed's analysis, in which the intricacy and reflection in shame diminishes and is replaced by a rallying cry of one group against another. Probyn argues that shame works on a bodily level but, unlike empathy, does not allow for any easy sense of commonality, thus drawing an implicit distinction between the productive potential in shame and sentimentalism.

Melodrama

So far this chapter has focussed primarily on theorising the concepts of emotion and affect within feminist theory. The final section turns to work that bridges the gap between theorising emotion and studying it in relation to television and ethnography. Both examples, from research by Lila Abu-Lughod and Purnima Mankekar, come from the field of the anthropology of the media. In the introduction to their collection, *Media Worlds: Anthropology on New Terrain* (2002), editors Faye D. Ginsburg, Lila Abu-Lughod and Brian Larkin explain that anthropologists working in the media study 'the social fields that structure these engagements and the actual ways audiences engage with media' (2002: 13).

In her work on Egyptian melodramas, Lila Abu-Lughod considers 'how the representation of characters' emotions in Egyptian melodrama might provide a model for a new kind of individuated subject' (2002: 117). Abu-Lughod argues that in order to consider this 'one cannot simply analyse the overt messages of the plot and character, just as one should not limit oneself to the study of reception' (ibid.: 117). Interestingly, the woman she observes, 'Amira', makes 'herself the subject of her own life stories . . . Amira was the one whose tales most clearly took the form of melodrama' (ibid.: 123). Abu-Lughod finds that Amira imagines her own life to be part of a melodrama and explains her experiences accordingly. She has not only become emotionally involved with the characters of her favourite melodrama but has also adopted the structure of the melodrama in her discussions and imaginations of her own life. This 'melodramatic imagination', to borrow Peter Brook's phrase may lead, as Abu-Lughod suggests, to a more individuated subject – one 'appropriate for citizenship and perhaps consumerism' (ibid.: 129). In other words, the emphasis on personal feelings in melo-drama creates viewing subjects who value their own personal experi-ence and emotions, their own 'privatised worlds', as discussed in the previous chapter, so much so that they begin to imagine and construct their knowledge of the world in these terms.

Mankekar's *Screening Culture, Viewing Politics* (1999) moves towards a 'feminist ethnography of mass media' in recognising a woman view-er's ability to 'critique televisual discourses at the same time that they intimately engaged with them' (1999: 24). One of the women she interviewed, 'Aparna', told her that in order to learn from television one must 'have a particular *bhaav* (loosely, "feeling" or "emotion," although neither word quite captures the meaning) in one's heart' (ibid.: 24, author's italics). When Mankekar asked the woman what she meant – whether this emotion existed in someone's heart and was elic-ited by something touching or whether this was a mood created by something on screen – the woman replied that it was not so simple (ibid.: 24). She explained that it was something that developed both because she watched films more frequently and because she had grown older and had more experiences with which to relate to the characters on screen. As Mankekar explains:

> One had to surrender to the mood of what was being watched; to learn from it, one had to be immersed in that state of being. And one had to be at a point in one's life where what was watched made sense *intimately*, at a level beyond mere empathy. (ibid.: 25, author's italics)

Mankekar finds this model of emotional engagement in many of the women she interviews; she explains that: 'even as they deeply identified with the characters on television, even as they experienced profound *bhaav*, many viewers were *simultaneously* able to stand back and critique what they watched' (ibid.: 26, author's italics). Mankekar argues that we need to distinguish between an emotional involvement with a text and a critical one. She finds the women viewers able to do both at the same time – one does not exclude the other. Her research leads her to make profound statements not only on emotion and television but also on the critical awareness of subjects that are often perceived as uncritical of their own situation:

> Thus intense emotional involvement occurred *simultaneously* with a critical awareness that enabled some women to "see through" the narrative to the agenda of the state. At the same time, while many of the viewers I met seemed extremely aware of the power of the state, television, through *bhaav*, also informed them, in a frighteningly fundamental way, about their place in the world. They learned about their position as gendered subjects, and as Indians, from *bhaav* as it mediated their interpretations of television's discourses. (ibid.: 28, author's italics)

Bhaav, or intense emotion, enables the women to understand more about themselves, the state and their position within it. Not only do the viewers critique the programmes themselves (the director's work, the plot, the camera angles) but they can also 'see through' to the political agendas embedded in the story's narrative. And yet, *at the same time*, they find themselves emotionally drawn into the story and its characters, and experience a sense of connectedness to the world. Mankekar's work is crucial in light of the discussion in Chapters 2 and 3. Her research suggests that viewers can have an emotional *and* critical position on a televisual text simultaneously, which contradicts the assumption that emotion disables a critical position.

Conclusion

I have chosen to focus on specific concerns within this literature, such as 'the personal is the political', 'language as affect', and 'shame', not only to outline the shared issues raised within this literature but also to illustrate the constitutive links between this work and earlier feminist projects. There is a long history within feminist theory of trying to recover and recuperate images of mad, hysterical and overly emotional women. However, the point in these works is not simply to counterpoise 'emotional' with 'revolutionary' – these authors have learned that it is not enough simply to oppose existing models with new and empowered ones. Instead what they offer is a fundamental critique of the place of emotion in our everyday lives and the way in which affect works to inform and inspire action. Further, the attention to emotion and affect in these works offers a way of thinking about subjectivity that is not tied solely to the psyche. In other words, our actions are guided not just by what we think but also by how we feel and our bodily response to feelings. Finally, it is significant that many of the authors discussed here select different emotions and affects, such as anxiety, fear and disgust, in their appraisals. In so doing, they draw attention to the specificity of emotion which prevents us from thinking about emotion as a totalising force. Instead we are encouraged to think about the explicit ways in which each emotion affects the individual and the social and how this may shape our relationship to what we watch on screen.

Notes

1. Elspeth Probyn suggests that Alison Jaggar's article, 'Love and knowledge: emotion in feminist epistemology' (1992 [1989]), was one of the first to consider what emotion might mean for feminism (Probyn 2005: 8).
2. See also: Chodorow 1999; Evans and Cruse 2004; Goldie 2000; Matravers 1998; and Peterson 2004.
3. Ngai draws attention to the definition of emotion and affect offered by Brian Massumi and Lawrence Grossberg. Grossberg (1992), for instance, writes: 'Unlike emotions, affective states are neither structured narratively nor organised in response to our interpretations of situations' (cited in Ngai 2005: 24–5). See also Berlant and Warner 2000.
4. The link between Cvetkovich's work and Berlant's is not surprising given that Cvetkovich was a participant in Berlant's 'Public Feelings' group (see Whilde 2007: 98).
5. In *The Interpretation of the Flesh: Freud and Femininity*, Brennan argues that 'misapprehensions about hysteria are themselves instances of the tendency to split biological or physical inquiry (real things) from psychosocial explanation (not real things)' (1992: 3). See also Kirby 1997.
6. See also Ahmed 2006 and her forthcoming work on happiness in which she continues to develop and expand her model of affective contagion (Ahmed forthcoming).

Discussion

1. Consider the various models of emotion and affect raised in this chapter. In what ways are they useful to a study of film and television?

2. Why do you think the concept of shame is the most discussed emotion in feminist engagements?
3. Consider Mankekar's explanation of '*bhaav*'; do you understand the kind of engagement her respondent, 'Aparna', discusses? Do you agree that this kind of emotional engagement also critically enables subjects to learn more about their national identity? Provide examples.

Further reading

Abu-Lughod, Lila (2002), 'Egyptian Melodrama – Technology of the Modern Subject?', in Faye Do Ginsburg, Lila Abu-Lughod and Brian Larkin (eds), *Media Worlds: Anthropology, on New Terrain*, Berkeley, CA: University of California Press, pp. 115–33.

Ahmed, Sara (2004), *The Cultural Politics of Emotion*, Edinburgh: Edinburgh University Press.

Berlant, Lauren (1997), *The Queen of America Goes to Washington City: Essays on Sex and Citizenship*, Durham, NC: Duke University Press.

Berlant, Lauren (ed.) (2000), *Intimacy*, Chicago, IL: The University of Chicago Press.

Brennan, Teresa (2004), *The Transmission of Affect*, Ithaca, NY: University of Cornell Press.

Cvetkovich, Ann (2003), *An Archive of Feelings: Trauma, Sexuality and Lesbian Public Cultures*, Durham, NC: Duke University Press.

Gunew, Sneja (2004), *Haunted Nations: The Colonial Dimensions of Multiculturalisms*, London: Routledge.

Mankekar, Purnima (1999), *Screening Culture, Viewing Politics: An Ethnography of Television, Womenhood and Nation in Postcolonial India*, Durham, NC: Duke University Press.

Ngai, Sianne (2005), *Ugly Feelings*, Cambridge, MA: Harvard University Press.

Probyn, Elspeth (2005), *Blush: Faces of Shame*, Minneapolis, MN: University of Minnesota Press.

Riley, Denise (2005), *Impersonal Passion: Language as Affect*, Durham, NC: Duke University Press.

Sedgwick, Eve Kosofsky (2003), *Touching Feeling: Affect, Pedagogy, Performativity*, Durham, NC: Duke University Press.

Thornham, Sue (2007), *Women, Feminism and Media*, Edinburgh: Edinburgh University Press.

Note for further study

Sneja Gunew coordinated an interdisciplinary team at the University of British Columbia, Canada (2005–6). The question addressed was: to what extent can we think meaningfully about affect outside the concepts and terms of European psychoanalysis? Monthly meetings culminated in a two-day colloquium with researchers from Australia, the USA and the UK. The workshop and symposium were captured in a DVD entitled *Feeling Multicultural: Decolonizing Affect Theory Colloquium*, (2007), Centre for Women's and Gender Studies, UBC.

5 Theorising Emotion in Film and Television

'Luke, trust your feelings' (*Star Wars*)

The last chapter critically reviewed the literature on emotion and affect primarily within feminist theory in order to outline some of the key developments in research on the concept of emotion. This chapter will turn to film theory, where the concept of emotion has been explored primarily through research by cognitive film theorists. Television is still a new area in terms of work on emotion and affect, so it is necessary to draw on theoretical ideas within film studies in order to think about how these ideas might be transposed to television studies. There are some obvious problems with the movement from film theory to television theory – such as differences in 'gaze', as Chapter 2 raised, or differences in audiences, as Chapter 1 considered, but alongside developments within cultural theory, as the last chapter discussed, this is the best way to work towards a model of how we can consider and evaluate the concept of emotion in television.

Two examples

In *Star Wars*, as Luke prepares himself to fire on the Death Star, Obi-wan Kenobi encourages him to 'trust his feelings'; it is an iconic moment and precedes the rebel victory over the 'dark side' of the force. Obi-wan's insistence that Luke 'trust his feelings' instead of the computer targeting system privileges gut instinct over scientific/ technical accuracy and gives feelings/emotions new significance. Indeed the whole series emphasises the powerful role feelings play in our lives.

In the reality television programme, *X-Factor*, tears are central to developing the persona of the competing contestants. For instance, in an episode where a final twelve contestants are chosen, tears and the ability to manufacture them instantaneously seem to guarantee one's place on the show. The camera moves in on each contestant's face as they explain their rationale for wanting to make it to the next stage and we, as the viewer, can almost guess who will make it through depending on how much they cry.

These two examples present some of the difficulties in theorising the concept of emotion in television and film because emotion functions differently depending on the genre, the narration, the writing, the production et al. Crucially, it could also be said that it depends on the *quality* of the text. But what makes good television? This chapter will consider the quality debate within television studies as a way of working towards how we might theorise emotion in television.

Television aesthetics and the quality debate

In his lecture on 'Broadcast television and the social contract' (1992) Thomas Elsaesser discusses the developments with British television that have led to a very different television aesthetics from those we might find in the USA. He begins by reminding us that film studies was more influential in setting an agenda for television studies than television studies itself. Because film studies was already established, television studies initially drew from the concerns raised within film studies and – even more importantly perhaps – used the same theoretical frameworks within film studies: namely, psychoanalysis, semiotics and gender studies.

Although this helped to establish some agendas within television studies, it also, as Elsaesser points out, created some problems – such as how we study individual texts or 'programmes', how we focus on audiences or institutions, how we think about something like 'auteur' studies in terms of television with its team-driven writing teams (and the differences between these writing teams in the USA and the UK). Although there are obvious problems with taking film theory and transposing it to television studies, it is still the most useful place to go when thinking about how to theorise events, concepts or ideas in television.

Elsaesser suggests that the demand for 'Quality TV' can be seen as a throwback to public broadcasting or as a code word for letting the current TV establishment continue to have their way and therefore to keep independents at bay – to retain control over the television landscape. This demand leads Elsaesser to guess at what the future of television might look like:

1. a terrestrial public service TV
2. quality TV as a luxury good
3. popular TV, meaning cheap TV, tabloid TV, much by satellite with fierce ratings wars (1992: 7–8).

Elsaesser argued these points in 1992. Almost two decades later, we can see the veracity in his predictions and can begin to appreciate why the 'quality debate' has become an important issue within television studies.

'Must See TV', as Jancovich and Lyons write in their introduction to *Quality Popular Television*, are 'programmes [that] have also been referred to as "date" or "appointment" television programming, and they are distinguished by the compulsive viewing practices of dedicated audiences who organise their schedules around these shows' (2003: 2). And yet, as discussed, new viewing practices mean that people are no longer changing their schedules to watch television. Why do we watch some programmes and not others? Without always being aware of it, we, as television viewers, continually make aesthetic judgements about the shows we watch, without necessarily having criteria through which we can judge why we like some things and not others. As Bird contends: 'We know that all popular TV is not equal in quality, yet we cannot define what quality is, so we fall back on questions of popularity and ideology' (2003: 142). At the end of her 1990 article 'Problems with quality', Charlotte Brunsdon states: 'Judgements are being made – let's talk about them' (1997: 147). More than a decade later, Christine Geraghty (2003) attempts to develop some aesthetic criteria through which we can be more explicit about the judgements we invariably make.

Geraghty's purpose in considering the issue of quality on popular television is not only to establish a more transparent method through which we might judge what makes a television programme 'good' and another 'bad' but also to indicate how having a more defined criteria will help students and teachers improve their understanding of television. The second point is a fundamental one given that students today are the future television writers and producers. As Geraghty does well to point out, the lack of aesthetic criteria and emphasis instead on representation and ideology within television studies has led to a crucial difference between film studies and television studies: students have a 'passionate desire' to *make* films but have a 'passionate desire' to *be on* television, not to make television programmes (2003: 31). In my experience, students give very straightforward answers to 'what is your favourite television programme?' but lack a clear sense of why they like some shows and dislike others.

In order to address this problem, Geraghty proposes that we consider TV writing, sound, acting, characterisation,[1] and innovation as ways of evaluating television texts, and adds that 'individual writers could be recognized and their work analyzed even when it is obscured by the serial/series format?. The British examples she cites include:

Caroline Aherne, Paul Abbott, Tony Jordan, Debbie Horsfield and Kay Mellor (ibid.: 34). Geraghty argues that part of the problem of finding better ways to judge quality in television lies in better defining the criteria we use. She writes: 'Again there are different modes to be assessed – the wide range of dialogue in soaps, for instance, taking into account the use of regional accents, demotic references, emotional explosions and expository narrative statements' (ibid.: 34). 'Emotional explosions', as Geraghty refers to them, seem a useful way to begin thinking about how emotion is constructed in television.

Through his close examination of the drama genre, Robin Nelson poses similar questions around our judgements of television in *TV Drama in Transition* (1997). Like Geraghty, Nelson agrees that we 'make distinctions of worth all the time' (Nelson 1997: 218), whether we are aware of this or not. Following his reading of Wittgenstein's notion of knowledge through experience (ibid.: 225) Nelson argues that:

> Estimations of quality always come from somewhere: they are grounded in people's lived experience and people inhabit different places. Thus, there is always a significant proportion of ascription in people's aesthetic judgements, informed by their ethical and socio-political positions. (ibid.: 225)

Invoking Rorty, Nelson further argues

> that communicability of thoughts and feelings is possible though not foolproof, and that the roles of symbolic formations in bridging the gap between subjectivities is likely to be a significant one, on the contested ground of what it means to be human. (ibid.: 229)

In other words, Nelson argues for an 'engagement of emotion', by which he means to stress the fact that viewers think more reflectively and more intensely about human life (ibid.: 230).

There are of course problems with this model of aesthetics and Geraghty picks up on these in her critique of Nelson. Hindered by the scope of her article, Geraghty only briefly comments on Nelson's proposition, largely dismissing it by pointing out that his criteria is 'rational' and 'political' instead of aesthetic and arguing that 'he has ended up with a version of the "difficult", male-orientated, naturalist drama of an earlier television studies' (Geraghty 2003: 32). The implication in Geraghty's critique is that Nelson is more worried about the loss of programmes he enjoys instead of offering a grounded approach to aesthetics in television. Geraghty's analysis, however, is too brief and does not take into account programmes such as Mellor's and Abbott's which do engage with Nelson's ideals of a humanistic approach. However, Geraghty is right to point out, as she does in an endnote, that Nelson's model would be difficult to test in terms of audience research (Geraght 2003: 42, endnote 1). Judging how viewers reflect and ponder human life is hard to measure, although more and more research is attempting to define these terms, such as Bird's work on *Dr Quinn, Medicine Woman* (2003) and Robyn Warhol's work in *Having a Good Cry* (2003). For instance, Bird argues that 'perhaps the most dominant form of aesthetic appraisal is that known as emotionalism – a theory that emphasizes the expressive qualities of the object. How well does it communicate moods, feelings, and ideas?' (Bird 2003: 136) and attempts to answer this proposition through her ethnographic work on chat forums dedicated to *Dr Quinn, Medicine Woman*.

Nelson returns to the idea of 'quality TV' or what he refers to as 'high-end TV' in *State of Play: Contemporary 'High-End' TV Drama* (2007) and considers television programmes in terms of the text and its dramatic qualities and in terms of its visual and sonic presentation (2007: 26); in so doing he argues for the distinctiveness of certain texts such as *The Sopranos, Shooting the Past* and *Shameless*. While these qualities will be explored in more detail, particularly in relation to *The Sopranos* in Chapter 8, I want to draw attention to the way in which Nelson moves from a more abstract notion of humanism towards more concrete criteria for considering aesthetics and quality in television. In order to consider the concept of emotion in television it is necessary to move beyond generalised notions of 'feelings' towards specific elements in the text that elicit emotional responses.

Emotional audiences: theorising emotion in television

> Every story has got to make sense emotionally. When you get to love the main doctor, Christopher Eccleston, when he changes, then you will love him, then you will feel it happening, that's when regeneration works. When you feel it. (Davies 2005)

So how can we theorise emotion on television? As Davies points out, stories must make sense emotionally and allow you to *feel* their effect on you. Although there have been very few studies of emotion and television, there has been some important work that considers the relationship between feelings, emotion and cinema. Significantly, this work often engages with cognitive film theory rather than psychoanalysis, although some critics do rely on psychoanalytic accounts of emotion to develop their ideas, as will be explored at the end of this chapter.

In their assessment of psychoanalysis and film studies, Plantinga and Smith argue that:

The distinctions among pleasure, desire and emotion are not purely terminological. The choice of pleasure and desire over emotion is symptomatic (to use a Freudian term) of a larger theoretical neglect of the emotions. E. Ann Kaplan recognizes that psychoanalytic film theory's reticence about emotion has deep roots: "It was largely our anti-realism theory that made it difficult to use the word 'emotional' in recent feminist film theory: we have been comfortable with the 'cool', theoretical sounds of 'desire' . . . We were led to advocate a cerebral, non-emotional kind of text and corresponding spectator response. While discussing "desire" and "pleasure," psychoanalytic film theory could appear to be dealing with questions of emotion without having to pay closer attention to the specifics of emotional experience. (1999a: 11)

There are several things to draw from their assertion: first, the emphasis on desire and pleasure over emotions that Plantinga and Smith identify has shifted, and now there is more prominence within critical and cultural theory on emotion and affect, as the last chapter outlined. 'Desire' and the 'gaze', once 'cool' theoretical terms within feminist film theory have been called into question. In a special edition of *Signs*, 'Beyond the gaze: recent approaches to film feminisms', for instance, editors Kathleen McHugh and Vivian Sobchack argue that feminist film theory and media work is no longer dominated by psychoanalytic concepts such as 'the gaze' and 'desire'; instead, they believe that feminist film theory is 'an increasingly heterogeneous and dynamic set of concepts and practices' (2004: 1205). Although I have argued elsewhere that there is still a need to value the concept of desire within feminist film theory,[2] I have also suggested that there is a need to consider the emotional experience of spectators rather than place emphasis on a cool, detached or distanced response. The point worth making here is that distance must no longer be considered a necessary component to the spectator's critical response. The elision made between 'distance' and 'intellect' and 'closeness' and 'sentiment' needs to be challenged.

Indeed, there is very little feminist questioning of the distancing that is stressed in the process of identification within film studies. One of the only critiques of this distancing is offered within cognitive film approaches. As Plantinga argues, there is an assumption that 'social criticism or critical judgment must come through distancing and alienation' (1997: 384). Cognitive film theorists such as Carl Plantinga, Noël Carroll and Murray Smith rethink the concept of identification and use 'recognition' and 'emotional simulation' to describe the relationship between the spectator and screen. In *Engaging Characters: Fiction,*

Emotion and the Cinema (1995), for instance, Murray Smith suggests that the word 'identification', which is often used to describe the relationship between spectator and character, is less important than the model of the experience itself. He argues that we could also refer to words such as 'absorption' and 'empathy' to refer to the relationship that exists between spectator and character (1995: 1–2). Smith also distinguishes between the 'levels of engagement' and 'structures of sympathy' that exists within this model of experience. He refers to 'emotional simulation' as a way of explaining the process of identification, defining it as:

> observing the behaviour of a person in a certain situation about which we have limited knowledge – as is often the case with a character in fiction – we imaginatively project ourselves into their situation, and hypothesize as to the emotion(s) they are experiencing. (1995: 97)

The distinction that Smith makes allows us to concentrate on the emotions and affects the character's situation may have on the spectator. The emphasis on emotion and affect shifts the focus away from individual characters, and problematises any notion of 'overidentification'. In the cognitive model, spectators relate to the emotions the characters experience rather than identity with the characters themselves.

Cognitive film theory and emotion

In *Moving Pictures: A New Theory of Film Genres, Feelings, and Cognition* (1997) Torben Grodal argues that there are two lines of thought when it comes to theorising emotion: cognitive film theory and William James. William James posed the question 'What is an emotion?' over a hundred years ago. Robert Solomon begins his excellent collection on classic and contemporary readings of emotion with James's question, remarking that ever since James uttered this in the British journal *Mind* people have been debating and revising their answers (Solomon 1984: 1). In their introduction to their collection entitled *Passionate Views: Film, Cognition and Emotion*, Carl Plantinga and Greg M. Smith argue that 'cognitivists emphasise the way that emotions and cognitions cooperate to orient us in our environment and to make certain objects more salient. Emotions help us to evaluate our world and react to it more quickly' (1999a: 2). Plantinga and Smith's collection allows us to begin thinking about how emotion might be valued and discussed on screen.

In the first chapter of *Passionate Views*, Noël Carroll considers what he refers to as 'garden-variety emotions' – those of anger, fear, sorrow – and notes how emotion is structured by filmmakers. He argues that:

The filmmakers have selected out the details of the scene or sequence that they think are emotively significant and thrust them, so to speak, in our faces. The means that the filmmakers have to secure this end (sic) include camera position and composition, editing, lighting, the use of color, and of course, acting and the very structure of the script or narrative. (1999: 29)

This leads Carroll to suggest that it is possible to 'pith the emotive structure of the film', which means 'finding the aspects of the depictions or descriptions of the object of the emotion that satisfy the necessary criteria for being in whatever emotional state the audience is in' (ibid.: 33). Carroll argues that, in order to analyse the way a film arouses emotion, one must first determine the way in which the film is 'criterially prefocused'. In order to do this, the critic must think about the overwhelming emotion the film elicits, and then review how this emotion is constructed.

Carroll also argues that certain genres elicit specific emotions and he takes the suspense, horror and melodrama as examples. At the same time, in Linda Williams's 'Film bodies: gender, genre, and excess' she argues that what brackets genres such as the melodrama, the horror film and pornography from others is their 'apparent lack of proper aesthetic distance, a sense of over-involvement in sensation and emotion. We feel manipulated by these texts – an impression that the very colloquialisms of "tear jerker" and "fear jerker" express' (1991: 5). As Williams points out, these texts' ability to 'jerk' emotion from us lead to their cultural devaluation and to the perception that they are not 'good' for us, and, I would argue, a sense that we should feel ashamed or even angry if they have managed to make us cry or scream. Indeed, one of the problems with Carroll's notion of 'prefocusing' is that not all audiences will choose the same emotion as dominant in a particular text. Carroll himself suggests this when he concludes that: 'Through criterial prefocusing we could say that the filmmaker leads the horse to water. But the circuit is not completed until the audience drinks' (1999: 47). The audience must 'drink' the emotion the critic has prefocused, which might not always be the case. Because television programmes work through an episodic structure, it is more difficult to 'pith' the emotional structure of a series. Increasingly television programmes are more 'hybrid' in their structures and can contain elements of horror and melodrama across the series. However, it is still possible, and indeed probable, that audiences would identify some programmes as melodrama, such as *Grey's Anatomy* (ABC 2005–) and expect to cry at some episodes, while they would not think to consider an emotional dimension to a television programme such as *Top Gear* (BBC 1978–). Still, Carroll's notion that we must look for the dimensions of the text that elicit certain emotions can be applied to television and are in line with Nelson's approach to studying 'high-end' television drama.

Greg M. Smith approaches emotion through 'mood-cues'. He argues that '[t]he orienting function of emotion encourages us to seek out environmental cues that confirm our internal state' (1999: 113). So if we are feeling sad, we may gravitate towards watching a melodrama or if we are feeling energetic we might choose an action film. Our mood, in other words, orientates us towards certain films that we believe will match our internal feelings. This idea works particularly well in terms of thinking about how we orientate ourselves to an 'anchoring point' such as the television, although genres might not be as clearly defined in television as they are in cinema – viewers often know what will make them laugh, cry or scream. Smith also refers to what he calls 'emotion markers': 'configurations of highly visible textual cues for the primary purpose of eliciting brief moments of emotion' (ibid.: 118). These 'emotional markers' encourage and reinforce the mood of the viewer. Similar to Geraghty's 'emotional explosions', emotional markers are moments in the text of intense emotion that serve to continue the mood of the film. Smith expands on his idea of mood-cues in his book-length study of emotion and film entitled *Film Structure and the Emotion System* (2003). In the introduction, Smith reminds us that 'Films offer invitations to feel. Film audiences can accept the invitation and experience some of the range of feelings proffered by the text, or they can reject the film's invitation' (2003: 12). Smith's point is an important one as film or television does not *make* viewers feel, rather, we, as viewers, are *invited* to feel and must possess some level of understanding in order to make sense of the mood-cues we are offered. As Smith suggests: 'To accept the invitation, [to feel] one must be an "educated viewer" who has the prerequisite skills required to read the emotion cues' (ibid.: 12). This ability to 'read' the emotion cues can present some problems when we transport these ideas to television serials. Long-running story arcs may deliver emotional cues along the way, but only a faithful viewer will experience the full emotional impact of a well-crafted story arc. Smith examines a season of ITV's *Cold Feet* (Granada 1997–2003) as a way of considering how its handling of two emotionally moving storylines distinguishes it as 'good television'. He points out that television has the added burden of pacing its story through arc and episode: if a story is delivered too quickly it may exhaust the plot, if it is given too slowly, viewers might lose interest (2006: 84).

Jeff Smith begins his work on 'movie music as moving music' by reflecting on the final scene of David Lynch's *The Elephant Man* (1980). He wonders whether it is the character's plight or the music that accompanies the scene, or a combination of both, that always moves him when he watches it. Drawing on a phenomenological account of music cognition Smith examines two processes known as polarization and affective congruence. As he points out:

> [In] polarization, the affective qualities of the music move the visuals toward one side or the other of a bipolar semantic differential scale. In affective congruence, the matching of musical and narrative affect heightens and intensifies the emotional qualities of the cinematic signifier such that they exceed those of the musical and visual components in themselves. (1999: 167)

It is not difficult to think of moments when television uses music to heighten and intensify the emotional qualities of a text. Indeed, programmes also rely on theme tunes to get viewers in the mood for the emotions they come to expect from the shows. The theme tune for *ER*, for instance, uses siren sounds and strong tones to set the viewer up for the drama it delivers. In contrast, *The Sopranos* uses a slow beat and repeats the words 'woke up this morning, got myself a gun' to reiterate the gangster theme of the show. The series also uses music to construct a mood or to counterpoise the banality of suburban life. Glen Creeber argues that '[*The Sopranos*'s] use of music frequently helps to create a mood and an atmosphere reminiscent of Coppola's famously languid pace; perhaps even echoing the classical eloquence of Nino Rota's memorable theme tune to *The Godfather*' (2004: 106). As Creeber points out, music is used consciously to create mood, to establish and re-establish the gangster theme and to draw in viewers to the world of *The Sopranos*.

In his work on the 'scene of empathy and the human face on film', Carl Plantinga argues that the face plays a crucial role in eliciting emotion from viewers. He also advances the notion that the emotion in the close-up shot can be contagious to its spectators. He explains that:

> Emotional contagion is the phenomenon of "catching" others' emotions or affective states . . . When our friends laugh and smile while telling us a story, we often laugh and smile in response even if we fail to see the humor in the story itself. (1999: 243)

Here we can see similarities to Brennan's and Ahmed's arguments about emotional contagion discussed in Chapter 4. Like Murray

Smith, Plantinga prefers to think about engagement rather than identification. He also believes that the term engagement 'allows for empathy and antipathy, sympathy and indifference, and certainly implies no melding of minds or identities' (ibid.: 244). Similar to Jeff Smith's reading of affective congruence in music, Plantinga argues that 'the conventional scene of empathy uses music for affective congruence and to encourage emotional contagion' (ibid.: 254). Music is often used to accompany a particularly poignant moment in television and can elicit emotion from the viewer.

Carl Plantinga, Greg M. Smith, Noël Carroll and Jeff Smith make use of cognitive film theory in order to advance theoretical ideas on film and emotion and in so doing offer a useful framework to begin thinking about television and emotion. Plantinga's emphasis on 'close-up' shots, Smith's work on music, Carroll's attention to affective dimensions of the text and Smith's mood-cues help us to consider how we might think about emotion and television.

More recently, Anne Jerslev draws on Tan's and Grodal's theories on emotion and cinema in her assessment of the 'emotional responses' to *The Lord of the Rings* trilogy. As part of the International Lord of the Rings Research Project (funded by the Danish Research Council and an Economic and Social Research Council [ESRC] grant), Jerslev's works draws on data from a questionnaire to examine the emotional engagements viewers had with the three films and finds that viewer's experiences are centred around emotion. Jerslev divides viewer's descriptions of the emotional engagement into two main categories: the fictional universe (of the text) and the making of it (2006: 206). Jerslev draws on the distinction Tan (1996) makes between 'fiction emotions' and 'artefact emotions' – or, between a film's 'surface structure' and its deep structure. The crucial point made here, as Jerslev notes, is that 'an awareness of the film as artefact should by no means only be distanciating but may, on the contrary, contribute to and even reinforce the emotional engagement' (Jerslev 2006: 212). Indeed, Jerslev's research suggests, contrary to the distinction that Tan makes between artefact and fiction emotions, that 'artefact emotions are as strong and intense as fiction emotions' (Jerslev 2006: 213). Jerslev's work not only illustrates the importance in considering the emotional dimensions of film but also indicates a move away from thinking that the viewer must be distant from the text in order to make an intellectual judgement. Her work moves away from Brechtian distanciation towards an appreciation of how emotion facilitates new discourses on aesthetic judgement.

Psychoanalytic approaches to emotion in film/television

In Ang's work on 'melodramatic identifications' (1996. 85) she argues that we as critics must remember that characters like Ally McBeal are fictional, and for that reason are designed to engage the viewer at the level of fantasy, not reality. Ang suggests that these characters 'do not function as role models but are symbolic realisations of feminine subject positions with which viewers can identify *in fantasy*' (ibid.: 92, author's italics). Fantasy is central to Ang's argument and she conceptualises fantasy within a psychoanalytic framework. That is, she does not understand fantasy to be an illusion but as a version of reality – as a fundamental aspect of human existence. She is also operating within post-structural theories on subjectivity, arguing that 'being a woman implies a never-ending *process* of becoming a feminine subject – no one subject position can ever cover satisfactorily all the problems and desires an individual woman encounters' (ibid.: 94). In other words, Ang argues that being a woman involves work and so fantasy or, in this case soap operas, offer women space to adopt impossible or socially unacceptable positions.[3]

In her criticism of *Dallas*, Ang argues that women are able to indulge in feelings otherwise 'unallowed'. Extending this logic to *Ally McBeal*, it can be argued that Ally, as a character, allows women to explore their feelings of anxiety about their position within a male-dominated workplace, about being thirty something and about marriage and having children. Ang argues that while watching soap operas women are allowed to pause their own self-construction: she calls these moments, 'moments of peace, of truth, of redemption, moments in which the complexity of the task of being a woman is fully realised and accepted' (ibid.: 95). In referring to these moments as 'truth' or as 'redemption' Ang seems to suggest that these 'unallowed' or 'socially impossible' positions are what women really want for themselves. Although I am sceptical that these 'moments' are shared by all women, I can appreciate that many women do experience a sense of escape while watching a show like *Ally McBeal*, and this is echoed in viewers' reactions to the show (see Hermes 2005; Gorton 2004).

Ang links the *pleasure* viewers take from watching serialized programmes such as *Dallas* with the 'ever-changing emotions' they find within the text. One of her respondents writes the following:

Now I'll tell you why I like watching *Dallas*. Here goes!
There is suspense in it.
It can also be romantic.

There is sadness in it.
And fear.
And happiness.
In short, there is simply everything in that film. (1985: 'letter 16', 45)

For Ang, this viewer's response typifies the 'structure of feeling' or what she refers to as the 'tragic structure of feeling' that underlines viewers' appreciation of the text and the pleasure they take from watching it. Ang adds 'tragic' to Williams' 'structure of feeling' (Williams 1977: 128–35; 1961) because she feels the text never fully supports the notion of happiness – any happiness in the text is always complicated or challenged which leads to the ups and downs, the emotional journey viewers enjoy so much. Indeed, feminist criticism on television programmes such as *Ally McBeal* and *Sex and the City* suggest that the ambivalence and contradiction inherent to these shows are responsible for their enduring popularity. In *Television and Sexuality* (2004), for instance, Jane Arthurs believes that:

> the widespread popular success of *Sex and the City* and *Ally McBeal* suggests that contradictory and unstable texts steeped in melodramatic and comedic excess are usable precisely because they allow people to explore the contradictions and instablities of their own subjectivity. (2004: 133–4).

Whether looking at texts such as *Sex and the City*, *Ally McBeal* or *Bridget Jones* from the position of their popularity, their presence within feminist theory or their appeal to viewers, theorists note the ambivalence and contradiction that mark them.

Towards a theorisation of emotion in television

This chapter has explored key concepts within television studies, cognitive film theory and psychoanalysis in order to consider how the concept of emotion can be valued and theorised in television. Moving away from generalised ideas of feelings towards formal qualities in the text, this chapter has considered how 'emotion markers', 'mood-cues', 'the scene of empathy', music, identification and empathy and aesthetic qualities work together to produce emotion.

The second half of the book will draw on the theoretical work outlined so far and use this research to consider specific case studies – on television writing, on the lifestyle/reality television genre, on 'quality tv' within feminist television criticism and, finally, within the television industry itself. These case studies begin to theorise how emotion is used, understood and valued within television. Although it is possible to study emotion in many television genres, such as news, sports, documentary and comedy, I have chosen to limit the case studies to a study of emotion in drama, soaps and reality/lifestyle television.

Notes

1. Bird's research demonstrates 'that a concern for coherent character development is central to appreciate of genres from TV to literature' (2003: 135).
2. For more information on Davies's work, see Nelson 2007: 78–85.
3. See Gorton 2004.

Exercises

Watch an episode of television – preferably something that you might consider 'emotional' (or watch something you would not consider 'emotional' so you can discuss the difference).

After viewing the programme, split into groups and consider the following questions:

- How is emotion constructed in the text?
- Do you identify with the characters or with the situations they are in (or both)? Following this, which model of emotion do you feel is more useful for an analysis of televisual texts?

Further reading

Geraghty, Christine (2003), 'Aesthetics and quality in popular television drama', *International Journal of Cultural Studies*, 6(1): 25–45.

Grodal, Troban (1997), *Moving Pictures: A New Theory of Film Genres, Feelings and Cognition*, Oxford: Oxford University Press.

Jerslev, Anne (2006), 'Sacred viewing: emotional responses to *The Lord of the Rings*', in Ernest Mathjis (ed.), *The Lord of the Rings: Popular Culture in Global Context*, London and New York: Wallflower Press, pp. 206–24.

Nelson, Robin (1997), *TV Drama in Transition: Forms, Values and Cultural Change*, Basingstoke: Macmillan, now Palgrave Macmillan.

Plantinga, Carl and Greg M. Smith (1999b) *Passionate Views: Film, Cognition and Emotion*, Baltimore, MD: The Johns Hopkins University Press.

Smith, Greg M. (2003), *Film Structure and the Emotional System*, Cambridge: Cambridge University Press.

Smith, Greg M. (2006), 'A case of cold feet: serial narration and the character arc', *Journal of British Cinema and Television*, 3(1): 82–94.

Tan, Ed S. (1996), *Emotion and the Structure of Narrative Film: Film as an Emotion Machine*, Mahwah, NJ: Lawrence Erlbaum Associates.

Thorburn, David (2000), 'Television melodrama', in Horace Newcomb (ed.), *Television: The Critical View*, 6th edn, Oxford: Oxford University Press, pp. 595–608.

Part Two

Case studies

6 A Sentimental Journey: writing emotion in television

If I go to the cinema to watch something and I've not been moved
. . . and laughed out loud, I feel cheated really, to be honest with you,
that's part of the experience of going to the cinema and also when
I'm watching TV, I'm the most greedy television viewer that you
can think of, because I want everything, that's why I write like that,
because that's what I want, I want that journey.

(Kay Mellor 13/6/05)

In the introduction to *Passionate Views: Film, Cognition and Emotion*,
Carl Plantinga and Greg M. Smith remind us that one of the primary
reasons why people go to the cinema is to 'feel something' (1999a: 1).
Indeed, in an advertisement for FilmFour the voice-over reiterates this
notion by promising us that we, as viewers, will 'be moved' by moments
in the films they have chosen. A movie's ability to move audiences emotionally is crucial to their success, and yet, as Plantinga and Smith point
out, it is one of the least explored topics within film studies (1999a: 1).
This claim is even more apt for television studies, where a programme's
ability to 'move' audiences is not critically valued or discussed.

And yet, as Mellor suggests, people often go to the cinema or watch
television in order to experience a 'journey', one that provides an
emotional and intellectual engagement with the story that unfolds.
This emotional 'journey' is not just what makes a film or television
programme successful but it is also, I shall argue, what makes them
'good'. However, critical work on television continues to overlook or
disregard the value of emotion or sentiment within programmes.
Indeed, the sentimental or emotional programme is often perceived as
easy, constructed and simplistic and watched by a lazy audience.

As the first of the case studies on emotion in television, this chapter
considers the importance of writing to the construction of emotion in a
televisual text, by drawing in particular on an interview with British
television writer/producer Kay Mellor. Although there has been little
academic engagement with her work, Mellor is undoubtedly a major

television phenomenon: she has successfully written and directed a play, *A Passionate Woman* (1992); she has written and directed several award-winning comedy dramas, including *Fat Friends* (ITV, Rollem and Tiger Aspect 1999–), *Band of Gold* (Granada 1996), *Playing the Field* (Tiger Aspect for BBC 1995), *Between the Sheets* (ITV 2003); she has written and directed a movie, *Fanny and Elvis* (The Film Consortium 1999), for which she was awarded the Audience Award at the Dinard Film Festival; and she has her own production company, Rollem Productions, through which she has been able to retain creative control.

Her work might usefully be situated within the broader context of the British social realist tradition and reflects both the concerns inherent to this project and also the more recent shifts within it. As Samantha Lay argues in *British Social Realism*: 'social realist texts portraying working class lives increasingly do so by defining them in terms not of what they produce but rather what they consume' and, to a greater extent, 'how what they consume also consumes them' (2002: 105–6). Lay's critique can be easily applied to Mellor's work, particularly to one of her most recent drama series, *Fat Friends*. Centring on the lives of a group of overweight members of a Leed's 'slimming club', the series explores, among other issues, how 'you are what you eat'.

Given Mellor's status within the television industry, I found the scarcity of academic comment on her work – nothing more than a footnote on its quality[2] – surprising, a thought that led me to wonder if it was not the emotional intensity of her work that kept her texts from being critically analysed. I think it is more likely that the absence of academic writing on her work is because most of her television programmes are dismissed as 'middlebrow'. As Greg M. Smith argues: 'Our academic discussions frequently leave out the middlebrow, the vast number of popular culture forms between the high and the low' (2007: 6). Indeed, there is very little work on highly popular but decidedly middlebrow television programmes that are often lumped under the patronising heading of 'light entertainment'. Matt Hills suggests that one reason for this absence in television studies could be because these programmes are rarely offered on DVD and are therefore not often the subject of close analysis or academic attention (2007: 7).

And yet Mellor's work illustrates the idea that emotion can be viewed as an aesthetic quality, in that she must use formal devices to construct it within her work. And, at the same time, emotion is used to create empathy between characters and viewers which facilitates their understanding and interpretation of the programme. Mellor's comments also contradict the notion that the presence of sentimentalism in a text means that it is 'bad' television. In fact, the emotional engagement is part of what she considers to be a fundamental part of good television. As she argues:

> I think good television is engaging, it is as relevant to today as yesterday, I think it's something that has great characters, a good story, with a beginning, a middle and an end even if it's a series, that you feel a sense of satisfaction with watching just one episode of something. And I think it should involve an emotional journey and that should include laughter and tears, and if you can include knowledge as well . . . that's fantastic – a knowledgeable journey, a political journey . . . that's what I think is good television. (13/6/5)

Mellor cites both an emotional journey and a political one and the two are fused within her understanding of the way emotion is used in her work and work similar to hers. Her understanding goes against criticism that perceives emotional texts as uncritical ones. It also counterpoises assumptions made about popular programmes which place sentiment in opposition to 'good television'. Mellor's responses reiterate the idea that emotion can be viewed as an aesthetic quality, in that she must use formal devices to construct it within her work, and, at the same time, emotion is instrumental in its ability to create recognition between the viewer and screen.

In *The Audience in Everyday Life* (2003), S. Elizabeth Bird revisits debates about emotionalism and sentimentalism as legitimate aesthetic discriminators. In her exploration of the possibilities for a 'popular aesthetic', Bird engages with criticism of popular culture within cultural theory and argues that popular culture has largely been addressed either in terms of its popularity with audiences (ratings), its representation of minority issues (she offers 'race in *ER*' as an example), or in terms of audience response. As a result of these interests, the question regarding popular television's 'quality' is often overlooked. As she argues: 'for the most part . . . scholars do not care to define what is "wrong" with the middlebrow in terms of taste or aesthetic judgment; they just ignore it (2003: 121–2). Bird argues that 'perhaps the most dominant form of aesthetic appraisal is that known as emotionalism – a theory that emphasizes the expressive qualities of the object. How well does it communicate moods, feelings, and ideas?' (ibid.: 136). Similarly in *Having a Good Cry*, Robyn Warhol examines how it *feels* from a viewer's perspective to watch a soap and to become emotionally involved with a series and finds that the audience experience emotion in different wave patterns than the narrative would suggest – an experience which Warhol refers to as an 'undertow' of emotion (2003: 116–17). I suggested Warhol's term 'undertow' to Mellor and she agreed that: 'what's not said is often very important' (13/6/5). Mellor's attention both to the speaking and not-speaking is crucial to developing the empathy viewers experience with her characters. Watching them listening instead of talking builds tension which allows viewers a sense of release through an 'emotional explosion'. As Mellor discusses:

> If you create a character that you empathise with, you'll go with that character, therefore you can say anything you want, you have more flexibility to say what you want as a playwright if you empathise with a character. So, for instance, 'Betty' in both the play and the television series that I wrote . . . was a woman who was very reserved and didn't say what she felt and we [are] constantly left feeling: 'Why don't you say something?' . . . and that's what I wanted my audience to feel, that they wanted her to speak out. So ultimately when she does speak out it creates a great cathartic experience within us because we feel it with her: therefore then, she speaks for us. (Mellor 13/6/5)

Mellor refers to the emotional journey that she builds into the narrative and the characters. Creating a tension within the character and within the situation not only allows for good drama but also allows for a release on the part of the audience. In order to construct this journey Mellor emphasises formal devices such as close-up shots and close attention to the actor's face. As discussed in Chapter 5, Carl Plantinga refers to this as the 'scene of empathy' (1999: 239) and it is clear that the use of close-up shots facilitates the audience's empathy with the characters. As Mellor argues: 'I want people to be able to get to know the character's quickly and what better way than the face' (13/6/5). She also adds that:

> as a writer and as producer/director you use close-ups on the characters a lot, particularly at times when [the character doesn't] speak . . . I always ask for the shot of her or him listening . . . I'm more interested in listening than I am in speaking because the effect that it has on what someone is saying is ultimately really important. (13/6/5)

Mellor reveals a conscious use of emotion within her work as a means of creating empathy between viewer and screen. And yet she is also careful not to overuse this emotion and points towards a balance that must be achieved; she suggests that: 'sometimes we railroad through emotions and we sometimes need the emotion to resonate, permeate through the characters, to build emotion' (13/6/5).

As Chapter 5 outlined, cognitive film theorists place emphasis on certain formal qualities in the text that orient us toward certain emotions (1999b: 2). For this reason it is important to think about which characteristics of popular television elicit an emotional reaction from their viewer. Mellor suggests the following: 'Full face, writing, music . . . Silence . . . and casting . . . You need actors who can understand the kind of emotional depth you're trying to bring across' (13/6/05). In speaking with Mellor, it is clear that emotion is built into the text through these formal devices, but it also became evident that her use of emotion creates a sense of recognition between viewer and screen. As Carl Plantinga argues in his work on spectator emotion:

> In mainstream films, allegiances with and antipathy toward characters orient us. What we are oriented *toward*, and respond to, are characters in narrative situations. Emotional response both inside and outside the theatre depends in part on our evaluation of a situation or scenario. (1997: 381, author's italics)

In other words, we, as viewers, are oriented or drawn to the expressive qualities of the text, the emotional situation that the characters are involved in. Murray Smith's model of emotional engagement shares commonalities with sentimentalism and lends itself to a sense of aesthetics that can help us to reconsider the role emotion plays within television studies. As Mellor argues, this emotional engagement with characters is partly what allows viewers to make sense of what they watch:

> I think it's the job of the playwright to elicit emotion from the reader or the viewer. I think that's part of the journey of good drama; you need to create empathy and sympathy for your characters and once you've done that you can travel with them wherever, you feel like you know them, when somebody breaks down in front of you, or makes themselves vulnerable in front of you, you feel that much closer to them . . . (13/6/5)

Mellor clearly identifies empathy as a fundamental aspect in creating a connection between viewer and screen. It is what allows us, as viewers, to *know* the characters, to understand them and furthermore to interpret their significance in relation to the narrative of the programme.[3] In her study on emotion and art, Jenefer Robinson refers to this process as a 'sentimental education' and argues that: 'The reader watches the education of the characters' emotions, and is thereby given a lesson in how the emotions function as teachers' (2005: 158). However, instead of interpreting this process as valuable and integral to the aesthetic appreciation of the text, it is often disregarded as contrived and uncritical.

Indeed, the assumption, made by theorists, that emotionalism in texts encourages passivity and uncritical distance also shares clear links with negative interpretations of sentimentalism.[4] But it is not just that the viewer enjoys or takes pleasure in this experience – it is also that this emotional engagement can be understood as part of the quality of the text. Viewers are able to distinguish what it is they like about these films and are critical of other films like them that do not achieve this emotional connection. This is crucial for audience studies, as discussed in Chapter 1, where there has been a long history of debate over whether the audience is passive or active, and the underlying implication in criticism of emotional or sentimental texts is that they have a passive and/or uncritical audience. Instead, recent research suggests that they are very active. Bird writes:

> Certainly both [*Dr Quinn*] and soap operas have been decried for their 'easy' sentimentality. Yet both sets of fans show that in this area too they are discriminating and active in the way they respond, usually connecting the emotional and expressive with the moral dimensions. (2003: 137)

Because these texts are associated with the sentimental there is an assumption that they are passive. As Knight argues: 'In short, according to the standard view, sentimentality leads us away from active, cognitive engagement with the ambiguities and complexities of the real . . . toward the over-simplified, the distorted, the falsified, the fantasized, the fictional' (1999: 417). As Knight suggests, the assumption is that the sentimental leads to the simplified, the uncomplicated and therefore to the passive viewer. However, as Knight's essay demonstrates so well, we need to question the assumptions that have been and continue to be made about sentimental texts and their audiencs' responses and recognise, as recent research has done, that these emotional texts are far from over-simplified and are therefore too important to be overlooked. As Bird argues: 'Dismissal of middlebrow shows as clichéd, sentimental schlock, often without watching them, is indeed elitist, depending heavily on easy social and gender-based stereotyping' (2003: 143).

A text's ability to move us emotionally is not simply an aesthetic value but also a political one. The presence of emotion in popular television moves its viewers to feel a sense of connectedness and belonging that is repeated in each episode. The repetition attaches them to the text: they often come to expect and even desire this engagement. As Sara Ahmed reminds us in her appraisal of emotions and cultural politics:

> Emotions are after all moving, even if they do not simply move between us. We should note that the word 'emotion' comes from Latin, *emovere*, referring to 'to move, to move out'. Of course,

emotions are not only about movement, they are also about attachments or about what connects us to this or that. (2004: 11)

Emotions connect viewers to a sense that relationships, whether in the
family, community, workplace, matter and that they will enable us to
cope with the everyday struggles and pressures of life. However, the
importance of emotion in these texts is not simply about allowing the
audience to feel 'better' or even 'moved'. As Martha Nussbaum poeti-
cally explains: 'emotions . . . involve judgements about important
things, judgements in which . . . we acknowledge our own neediness
and incompleteness before parts of the world that we do not fully
control' (2001: 19).

Nussbaum clarifies the movement in emotion that Ahmed refers to,
stressing that this movement is not about 'unthinking energies that
simply push the person around' (Nussbaum 2001: 24). Instead
Nussbaum argues that their relation to the object that draws them is
intentional and 'embodies a way of seeing' (ibid.: 27–8). Perhaps this is
the greatest value to the presence of emotion in popular television: it
allows for a way of seeing that is different from other viewing. It allows
viewers a chance to acknowledge their neediness while also feeling
connected to something outside them. As Mellor argues:

> I don't see the point of writing to be honest with you unless it moves
> . . . I think it's your job to do that, to hold a mirror up to society, to
> see the ridiculousness of the situation sometimes, to see the pain that
> people go through, along with humour too. I think humour is huge
> too and humour is also an emotion that we forget sometimes,
> putting that hand in hand is really important. (13/6/5)

Mellor understands her role as a television writer as someone who is
capable of reflecting societal issues in order to challenge and question
received views. 'Holding a mirror up to society' she reminds viewers
that they are not alone in the situations and emotions they experience.
This is important in terms of popular television in that it is often dismissed and overlooked, considered to be watched lazily and without
challenge by its audiences. There is an assumption, as discussed before,
that its viewers are passive in their appreciation, and yet, as research
suggests, they are able to make aesthetic and moral distinctions about
the programmes they follow.

In her reappraisal of sentimentalism, Warhol writes:

> To those who ask, 'What's "good" about "the good cry"?' I respond
> (without sarcasm, now) that the ideals of sentimental culture – the
> affirmation of community, the persistence of hopefulness and of

willingness, the belief that everyone matters, the sense that life has a purpose that can be traced to the links of affection between and among persons – are good ideals. (2003: 55–6).

What comes through in Mellor's work is 'the affirmation of community, the persistence of hope' and the 'belief that everyone matters'. These 'good ideals' structure her narratives and are made clear to the viewer through her characterisation and use of emotion. I would go further to argue that they are what make her programmes popular. The notion that 'everyone matters' is clearly an enjoyable message for viewers, but is also reflective of sentimental concerns. Furthermore, it suggests that emotionalism in television is not just there to provide escapism or light relief but is also needed as an art form that speaks to 'the links of affection between and among persons'.

What Mellor's work demonstrates is a sentimental engagement between spectator and screen that is not fantastical but is nonetheless effective and which provides an emotional simulation between character and viewer that may perhaps resonate more profoundly than previous understandings of emotional engagements have allowed. It reminds us that emotions are what endow characters with meaning and allow us, as viewers, to make sense of their significance for the story being told.

Mellor is not alone in both her use of emotion in television writing and her valuation of emotion as an aesthetic component of good television. In the Huw Wheldon lecture to the Royal Television Society in September 2005, 'What Do You Want to Watch Tomorrow?', Paul Abbott, whose successful television programmes include *Shameless* (Channel 4 2004–), *State of Play* (BBC 2003) and *Clocking Off* (BBC 2000–3), addressed concerns about the future of television by emphasising the need of writers to offer their audiences an emotional and political engagement. He argues that:

> Drama SHOULD (sic) reflect society, but Not so literally that we might as well just stand at a bus stop and get the same gig. We need more drama that unpeels society, that roots through the cubbyholes to fetch us nuggets of human behaviour that opens our eyes a bit. Not just the dark stuff. Wondrous fragments of ordinary people that can take our breath away. (2005)

Abbott's insistence that 'drama should reflect society' and 'open our eyes a bit' reiterates the need for a text to move its viewers. One of the ways in which a text is able to do this is through an emotional engagement between viewer and screen. He argues that: 'only by giving the viewer a workout, making them join the dots, use their own imagination, can we reclaim television drama as the challenging, exciting, life-changing medium that I and many others have known it to be' (2005).

When asked to consider what makes good television, Mellor and Abbott point to the importance of an emotional journey. They also share an understanding of how this emotion becomes reflective of society and therefore enables its viewers to connect with what they are watching in a more meaningful way. This connection counterpoises the assumptions made by critics that the sentimental viewer is lazy and incapable of making aesthetic judgements and should encourage us to reconsider how a sentimental journey is part of what makes good television.

This sentiment is echoed in Raymond Williams's work when he argues that:

> To succeed in art is to convey an experience to others in such a form that the experience is actively re-created – not 'contemplated' not 'examined' not passively received, but by response to the means, actually lived through, by those to whom it is offered. (1961: 51)

Williams recognised the importance of art to illustrate what he referred to as 'lived connectedness'. It is that 'lived connectedness', ordinary people and their creative capacity, that characterises 'middlebrow' texts and makes them so appealing to their audiences.

Knight warns us of the philosopher who dismisses sentimentalism as trivial and unimportant, and likewise we must be warned against dismissing 'middlebrow' television and losing its relevance within television studies and within an understanding of television aesthetics. There is a clear link here between the sort of philosopher Knight describes and the television critic who dismisses or excludes certain television writers. As she argues, what it really explains is the position the critic takes, the distanced, morally virtuous position instead of the researcher who tries to understand why these programmes, genres, are so successful and compelling to their audiences. Instead of questioning why people like these programmes, why they are 'happy while they weep', they are dismissed or glossed over.

Notes

1. *A Passionate Woman* opened to excellent reviews in 1992 at the West Yorkshire Playhouse. It was then transferred to the West End Comedy theatre where it ran for a year. It was subsequently followed by five national tours. Productions have also been held in Spain, Sweden, France, Australia, America, South Africa, Iceland, Finland, Austria and Poland.

2. The references to Mellor appear in Geraghty 2003, discussed in this chapter, and in Cooke 2003. Cooke notes that: 'the writer and actor Kay Mellor created a number of ensemble dramas with strong, independent female characters, including *Band of Gold* (Granada, 1995–6), *Playing the Field* (BBC1, 1998–) and *Fat Friends* (Yorkshire, 2000–)' (2003: 187).

3. In her explanation in the 'Importance of being emotional', Jenefer Robinson argues that our 'emotional responses to novels, plays, and movies help us to *understand* them, to understand characters, and grasp the significance of events in the plot' (2005: 105, author's italics).

4. For a brilliant appraisal and defence of sentimentalism, see Solomon 2004.

Discussion

1. Consider the difference between the concepts of 'emotion' and 'sentimentalism'. Critically discuss some of the negative associations the concept of 'sentimentalism' invokes.

2. How would you trace an 'emotional journey' in a television text?

3. This chapter has discussed work by Kay Mellor and Paul Abbott – what other television writers do you think value emotion in their work?

Further reading

Bird, S. Elizabeth (2003), *The Audience in Everyday Life: Living in a Media World*, New York: Routledge.

Bonner, Frances (2003), *Ordinary Television: Analyzing Popular TV*, London: Sage.

Carroll, Noël (1999), 'Film, emotion, and genre', in Carl Plantinga and Greg M. Smith (eds), *Passionate Views: Film, Cognition, and Emotion*, Baltimore, MD: The Johns Hopkins University Press, pp. 21–47.

Cooke, Lez (2003), *British Television Drama: A History*, London: British Film Institute.

Devlin-Glass, Frances (2001), 'More than a reader and less than a critic: literary authority and women's book-discussion groups', *Women's Studies International Forum*, 24(5): 571–85.

Lay, Samantha (2002), *British Social Realism: From Documentary to Brit Grit*, London: Wallflower Press.

McKee, A. (2001), 'Which is the best *Dr Who* story?', *Intensities: The Journal of Cult Media*, accessed online 18th October 2004 at http://www.cult-media. com/issue1/Amckee.htm

Mellor, Kay (1996), *A Passionate Woman: A Play by Kay Mellor*, London: Samuel French.

Nussbaum, Martha C. (2001), *Upheavals of Thought: The Intelligence of Emotions*, Cambridge: Cambridge University Press.

Solomon, Robert C. (2004), *In Defense of Sentimentality*, Oxford: Oxford University Press.

Warhol, Robyn (2003), *Having a Good Cry: Effeminate Feelings and Pop-Culture Forms*, Columbus, OH: The Ohio State University Press.

7 'There's No Place Like Home': emotional exposure, excess and empathy on TV

In *Restyling Factual TV*, discussed in Chapter 1, Annette Hill argues that if viewers relate to people in certain programmes, then the way they view themselves and their experiences change. 'When viewers witness the "ordinary drive of life" in reality programmes, they are immersed in the experience of watching and also reflecting on how this relates to them, storing information and ideas, collecting generic material along the way' (2007: 106). She goes on to suggest that: 'The most dominant response to *Wife Swap* is to mirror the judgemental attitudes of the participants' (ibid: 198); 'In this respect, participants in *Wife Swap* often let their emotions out and damn the consequences' (ibid.: 199). As the last chapter considered, one reason to watch film and television is to be moved. But how does emotion function in television, how is it *fashioned* by producers to elicit a response from the audience and what role does it play in our moral judgements of what we watch?

Charlotte Brunsdon concludes her work on lifestyling Britain with the argument that: 'Lifestyle programs are replete with implicit and explicit aesthetic judgment, and television scholars need to make the case why some are better than others' (2004: 89–90). In this chapter I argue that emotion in television is used to direct viewers' aesthetic judgements and to privilege the notion of self-transformation. Through an interdisciplinary reading of some recent work on the concept of emotion, discussed in Chapters 3 and 4, I consider how emotion functions within reality and lifestyle television. I argue that emotion is sometimes used as a social tool in a way that obscures differences of class, gender and race. Thus, while superficially operating as light entertainment, many reality or lifestyle programmes such as *Wife Swap* (Channel 4 2003–) seek legitimacy through a suggestion that they play a deeper pedagogic role: they invite us, the audience, to reflect on our intimate feelings and relationships through an empathetic engagement with the participants. Using devices such as the 'video diary' and the staging of final meetings between participants, programmes such as this use emotion as a tool to suggest that differences of class, race, sexuality and gender can easily be overcome through the emotional medium of a 'good cry'. Indeed, *Wife Swap* fashions emotional responses as a way of overcoming difference between the participants and between viewers and participants, thus eliding difference between women at the same time as reinforcing gender difference between the sexes.

One of the operating premises of the show is that it teaches its participants a variety of lessons: about themselves; about their parenting skills (or lack thereof); about their relationships – and in turn, we as viewers are offered the illusion that we too learn from their mistakes, bad judgements and excessive reactions. Central to this learning process is emotion, and it is implied that highly charged and intimate circumstances can operate for the public good. I question this implication through a discussion both of how emotions are mediated by the television screen and of the mechanisms by which these emotions of self-becoming become contagious.

One of the catchy aspects of programmes such as *Wife Swap* is the notion that distances and differences can be overcome through emotional exposure. That a simple case of walking in another's shoes could lead to self-transformation, self-actualisation and community. The reality, however, is that this visualisation of a utopian togetherness ends with the programme. What the wives and the rest of the family tend to realise is that there is no place like home. Emotion underpins this recognition and moves it along in an uncritical direction: we are not encouraged to trouble the notions of 'home' and 'family' with which we are presented, we are not prompted to question why the programme's title salaciously refers to a sexual practice and yet there is almost never anything sexy about the swap, and we are not asked to think about the ways in which the programme returns us to very conservative notions of home and family. Most often viewers watch and think themselves superior, or laugh or cry along with the participants. More importantly, perhaps, viewers are reassured that there is no place like their home, their wives/husbands and their way of doing things.

Consequently, I suggest that programmes such as *Wife Swap* play an ideological role in establishing notions of 'home' and in transmitting the emotions we should associate with 'home'. Indeed, while the possibility of any fundamental change is negated, we are offered the option of minor reforms of our existing lifestyles: we might spend more time with the kids, eat more vegetables, clean less frequently etc., but we are inhibited from seeing beyond the naturalised family structure. This minor shift is presented as pivotal (through the emphasis on emotional engagement between the couples) and leaves viewers feeling that a journey in someone else's shoes (or with someone else's husband/ wife) holds the potential for social harmony.

Contagious emotions

The notion that emotions are contagious has been developed by a number of theorists, and can be linked to Silvan Tomkins's work on affect, as discussed in Chapter 4. In his work, Tomkins designates affects as a primary motivational system and considers shame, interest, surprise, joy, anger, fear, distress and disgust as the basic set of affects (Tomkins 1995: 5). This idea has been picked up and developed in recent work on emotion and affect, such as in Teresa Brennan's *Transmission of Affect* (2004). Brennan argues that an increase in the perceived 'catchiness' of emotions 'makes the Western individual especially more concerned with securing a private fortress, personal boundaries, against the unsolicited emotional intrusions of the other' (2004: 15). According to Brennan, as people fear the emotional intrusions of the other, they begin to retreat and fortify their surroundings. It might reasonably be argued that one aspect of this process is the rise of lifestyle programmes that help foster a tendency towards people creating their own sense of home. In this chapter I am interested in how this move homewards means that there is more reason to think about the use of emotion on television.' Developing this suggestion, I am interested in thinking about how specific emotions, such as shame, happiness, anger and disgust circulate within media texts and attach themselves to concepts such as 'home' and 'wife' in a way that suggests to their audiences what kind of relationship should be there.

The importance of individual feelings

Recent sociological literature on the concept of individualism, discussed in Chapter 3, including primarily the work of Anthony Giddens (1990, 1991), Ulrich Beck and Elisabeth Beck-Gernsheim (2001) and Zygmunt Bauman (2001), illustrates the demand on the individual to be self-reflexive and to self-monitor and yet to be aware of the risks posed by modern society. This culture of individualism has given way to what Elliott and Lemert refer to as 'privatised worlds'. Elliott and Lemert chart a shift from a politicized culture to a privatised culture in order to consider the impact of 'reflexive individualism' and the way in which it places emphasis on 'choosing, changing and transforming' (2006: 97). The shift that Elliott and Lemert identify has also been the subject of work by Lauren Berlant, who argues that we increasingly live in 'an intimate public sphere'. According to Berlant the shift from a political public sphere to an intimate public sphere has led to a national politics that does not figure the nation in terms of the racial, economic and sexual inequalities that separate and divide the public; instead 'the dominant idea marketed by patriotic traditionalists is of a core nation whose survival depends on personal acts and identities performed in the intimate domains of the quotidian' (1997: 4). And what better place to perform these acts and identities than on television? Indeed, more recently, Berlant examines the way in which intimacy has increasingly been moved into the public domain and negotiated on our television screens. She argues, for instance, that 'in the U.S., therapy saturates the scene of intimacy, from psychoanalysis and twelve-step groups to girl talk, talk shows, and other witnessing genres' (Berlant 2000a: 1).

We can see the influence of the rise of individualisation on television, particularly in the popularity of 'reality' and lifestyle television. Rachel Moseley has identified the 'makeover takeover' that has affected British television and argues that: 'British makeover shows exploit television's potential for intimacy, familiarity, ordinariness and the radical destabilisation of the division between public and private' (2000: 313). In *Reality TV*, Anita Biressi and Heather Nunn refer to the 'revelation' side of reality programmes (2004) – which underlines the way in which programmes pivot around the final 'ta dah' moment, and, as Biressi and Nunn argue, can be seen as part of the key to the success of the reality genre (2004: 3). Indeed, Brunsdon charts a shift from a narrative of transformation around skill acquisition to one that emphasises the 'reveal'. As she writes: 'While contemporary lifestyle programs retain a didactic element, it is narratively subordinated to an instantaneous display of transformation' (2004: 80). Beverley Skeggs (2004), Helen Wood and Beverley Skeggs (2004) and Charlotte Brunsdon (2004) have all discussed the way in which lifestyle and reality television 'lifestyle Britain'. As Wood and Skeggs argue: 'choice mediates taste, displaying the success and failure of the self to make itself' (2004: 206).

Reality programmes underline an individual's ability to self-regulate, make choices, compete, monitor his/her performance and transform: examples include *Big Brother's* 'diary room' (Endemol 1999–), 'healthy competition' in *Survivor* (CBS 2000–; ITV 2001–), *Strictly Come Dancing* (BBC1 2004–), *The Biggest Loser* (NBC 2004–), and transformation in *10 years Younger* (Channel 4 2004–), *The Swan* (Fox 2004–5), *Extreme Makeover* (ABC 2002–7), *What Not to Wear* (BBC2 2001–4; BBC1 2004–). These programmes illustrate the emphasis placed on 'choosing, changing and transforming' that Elliott and Lemert identify as part of a self-reflexive individualist society. As they argue: 'The main legacy of this cultural trend is that individuals are increasingly expected to produce context for themselves. The designing of a life, of a self-project, is deeply rooted as both social norm and cultural obligation' (Elliott and Lemert 2006: 13). As Elliott and Lemert suggest, individual choice and self-transformation have become a cultural imperative and this demand is evident in the format and content of reality and lifestyle television.

Wife Swap

Part of what I want to argue in drawing attention to *Wife Swap* is that 'real' women are offered the chance to leave the fixity of their position as 'wife' to one family in order to take up a position as 'wife' to another. In the end, their feelings about their experience are used to grant them a transformation or becoming. However, their 'choices' are limited and stand in contrast to the notion of lifestyle freedom. Whether they clean all the time or never at all is constructed as a 'choice' and detracts from the real choices they may or may not be able to make. Emotion is used to draw us into these dilemmas and to fashion the viewer's response.

Wife Swap first aired in 2002 on Channel 4. It is now in its sixth series and, in late 2004, an American version was produced on ABC, and a spin off called *Trading Spouses* aired on the Fox network. *Wife Swap* won a BAFTA for Best Features in 2004 for the way it supposedly 'lifts the lid on how families live today'. The series follows a very basic format that is repeated weekly using different women. Each woman is asked to prepare a 'household manual' and is asked to respond to the following categories: Household Chores, Who do the following, and how often? (questions range from ironing to cleaning the bathroom), Cooking/Meals, Daily Routine, Childcare/Discipline, The Relationship and House Philosophy. The manual is left in the house for the other wife to follow. The use of a 'manual' illustrates what Angela McRobbie refers to as 'female individualisation' (2004: 260). Drawing on the concept of individualism as discussed in Giddens (1991), Beck and Beck-Gernsheim (2001) and Bauman (2001), McRobbie considers the way in which 'individuals must now choose the kind of life they want to live. Girls must have a lifeplan' (2004: 261). In many ways the 'manual' becomes this 'lifeplan' in the way it dictates and advises the other 'wife' to live.

Wife Swap generally pairs women who are very different from each other; either in terms of their class, their attitudes towards their careers, their children, their partners or all the above. The notion of lifestyles underlines the programme and the household manual itself.

The women are allowed to survey their new homes for the first time without anyone else around. The camera follows them as they observe the cleanliness or décor of their new home. Judgements are always made: whether the new wife is disgusted by the messiness of the place or happy at the size of her new house. The camera also pays close attention to each woman's response to the household manual and the 'knee-jerk' reactions the women make about their 'other's' choices. The rest of the family then makes an appearance and is introduced to their new wife/mother. In the first week, the wives must strictly abide to the household manual and to the routine of the original wife. At the end of the week, however, each new wife is allowed to set new rules that radically alter the lifestyle of the family and assert her position as the 'new wife'. At the end of the experience both couples meet up in a public location (usually a pub or hotel). This is generally the time the viewers look forward to: and it is often the most emotionally charged part of the programme. Emotion is central to the programme, as producer Stephen Lambert (of RDF Media) argues:

> Like most great ideas, [*Wife Swap*] is a very simple one that appeals to an ancient and very powerful emotion – that the grass is greener on the other side. At some point in their lives, most people will have fantasised about having a sexy new partner, or living in a Posh-and-Beck's style mansion with servants. *Wife Swap* actually gives the swapees the chance to try this alternate life out for real. (cited in Webb 2003: 9–10)

And this is what we get in *Wife Swap* – differing wifely roles – whether the kind that gets up at 5.00 a.m. and cleans or the kind that sits back and lets her husband do the work. There is a sense now that women are able to choose for themselves – and yet in *Wife Swap* the underlying implication is that the choice is a matter of choosing what kind of wife you are. What this does is place responsibility on the individual and her lifestyle choices, thus evading issues of class, gender, race and sexuality. As Skeggs argues: 'Attempts by the state to deflect attention away from class inequalities, through rhetorical signs of "lone mother", "smoker", "unhealthy school", create moral divisions between worthy and unworthy recipients, the respectable and good citizen and the socially irresponsible and excluded' (2004: 60). What we are offered are images of the 'good' mother/wife and the morally suspect one. As viewers, we can decide whose 'side' we are on (if any).

What is at play here is exposure (both of an imagined reality and of people's emotional states). In certain ways *Wife Swap* can be read in terms of the work that has been done on the 'reveal' side of television as the programme incorporates this anticipation into its structure, setting up the audience to wait and see what will happen when these two wives finally meet each other. But the final revelation offers an emotional transformation, not a physical one. When the two couples get together it is to reveal what has been kept secret (the time they were away from each other). Each couple serves as witness to how the events are narrated and to the various revelations each person has undergone. This is usually gendered: the men sit back and watch while their female counterparts yell and scream, thus reiterating a traditional notion of man as possessing self-control and rational thought and of woman as emotionally irrational and lacking self control. Close-up shots are also used to emphasise the importance of the emotional transformation each participant undergoes, particularly when the couples come together to discuss their experiences. The camera pans in on the participant's faces, eager to witness a tear or a look of disgust.

In season two, for instance, 'Lizzy and Emma' drew viewers' attention not only because Emma left her new home after only two days on the swap but also because their reunion scene was particularly caustic. The battle between them is clearly one of class (working class versus aspirational middle class) and each couple plays to their own stereotypes with impressive determination. After they argue with each other about their lifestyle differences, Lizzy makes a comment about Emma's morality, alluding to the fact that Emma and Colin began their relationship as an affair. The following exchange captures the emotional responses of all the participants:

> EMMA: When you fall madly in love with somebody you don't see logic or reason, you rule from the heart, and not the head. I would never, ever recommend anybody to see a married person, but unfortunately I was young and foolish, but now I think it's the best thing that I ever did.
>
> [long pause]
>
> LIZ: 'Your husband and your children are there with 'ya the majority of the day because of the lifestyle we've got, you love them and you tell them that you love them, but in such an extreme situation like this, you realise you love them even more [she begins to cry] . . . they are the most precious things to you, they're not your belongings, they yours.
>
> COLIN: That's the first time I've seen you with emotion this whole week Liz.

MARK: She is normal [laughs]. (Channel Four Television 2004)

At the end of this exchange 'happy' music begins to play and the two couples are filmed coming out of the main door and hugging each other. The lyrics 'Well I feel so good . . . I'm so glad we made it' from Steve Winwood's *Gimme Some Lovin* are played over the image of the couple's reconciliation and their return home. Music is used here to change the mood of the programme – to signal that the participants have overcome their differences and can now safely move towards a celebration of the emotional transformation that has occurred in both homes.

Audiences can read *Wife Swap* on many different levels. On one level, this is a programme designed for us to laugh at how weird people can be and how outrageous they can act. On another level, the pro-gramme clearly illustrates how divisive class continues to be. There is a third level on which to read this scene, however, and this is signalled by Emma's emotional disclosure and Lizzy's emotional response.

Emotion is illustrated here as something that brings people together, despite their class backgrounds, prejudice and hatred for each other. The moment Lizzy cries is figured as the pivotal moment and as the 'truth' of her feelings (although she may have acted tough and hostile before, deep down she's really insecure and loves her family – as her husband tells the other couple 'she *is* normal'). Lizzy's tears are figured as a sign of reconciliation and understanding. As Sara Ahmed suggests: 'the "signs" of emotion return us to the "promise" of community' (2004: 198). Here the dialogue of shaming between the two couples is framed as a necessary precursor to the emotional reconciliation. They must 'air' their anger in order to reach empathy. And empathy (in this case, understanding the other wife's way of doing things) is seen as capable of uniting disparate groups.

As with all the episodes, shortly after the meeting the voice-over tells us that 'two weeks later and there have been some big changes'. Almost without fail, our two wives, who generally have nothing but contempt for each other, decide that they will take on a few rule changes and 'learn' from the experience. Not only is there a transfor-mation in the wife, but also in the family – thus reiterating the wife's role as foundational. There is an implicit suggestion here of transfor-mation. The emotional experience has transformed these women into new and improved wives and we as viewers have learned which choices are good and which ones are bad. As Kirsty Fairclough writes: 'This humiliation is concealed in a veil of self-discovery for the participant and presumes that the audience will learn something from watching the misery and embarrassment of others' (2004: 346).

Emotional excess

The fact that the participants are real people (as opposed to fictional characters) heightens the sense that viewers are privy to intimate feelings and therefore there is a sense that this will increase an emphatic response. As the book that accompanies the series suggests:

> What is amazing about *Wife Swap* is that the people involved in the melodrama unfolding on the screen aren't actors, but members of the general public, living out their lives and discussing their most intimate thoughts in front of a camera . . . The camera as confessional is hardly a new concept, but in some cases it helped the viewers feel more sympathetic to the people involved, after seeing them express their most intimate feelings about the swap. (Webb 2003: 28)

As in melodrama, where emotion in the public domain creates a sense of excess, there is an excess produced by the feelings aired in the programme. As certain realities are exposed and the wife or husband is shamed ('you don't spend enough time with the kids', 'you don't do enough around the house' et al.) wounds are exposed but then neatly sutured – the families must return to their original wives even if the 'new' wife has 'worked' better. The constraints of television mean that the depth of the wounds cannot be fully dealt with and the format insists that we see progress (now the husband spends time with the kids, now the wife irons et al.). As a means of dealing with the excess this neat ending produces (and of capitalising on the popularity of the programme) the producers of *Wife Swap* created *Wife Swap: The Aftermath* for E4 in which both sets of wives, their husbands and families are videoed watching the premiere of their episode and then asked to comment separately on what they have observed. The programme extends the meeting session already incorporated within the original format, but this time includes sessions with a 'relationship expert' who tries to get an emotional response from the couples or asks them to reflect on their emotional responses to each other.

As the title suggests, *Aftermath* attempts to deal with the excess feelings that participants and viewers might have after *Wife Swap*. The fact that the advertisement for *Aftermath* appears just before the ending of *Wife Swap* emphasises its role in dealing with the unsaid and unanswerable of the original programme. *Aftermath* tempts the viewer by offering the promise that it will reveal what the participants really think about each other by placing them in another context – as viewers, not participants. The programme features the families on couches and chairs watching *Wife Swap* and commenting on the most emotional moments. Now viewers watch the participants as viewers watching themselves as participants – this sets up a mise en abyme which opens up a different kind of vicarious pleasure for the viewer at home. However, *Aftermath* does not deliver its promise to reveal participants' true feelings, instead it just extends the notion of judgement and lifestyle incorporated in *Wife Swap*.

Consequently, what happens in *Aftermath* is that an element of judgement is reintroduced. Because each family is filmed watching the episode and is positioned to comment on the other family, they are able to reflect on their own self-reflection, thus encouraging and reiterating the importance of 'choosing, changing and transformation'. It is not simply that they are asked to reflect, however, they are also led to judge and to assess their choices in relation to their counterparts. By acting as mediators, the programme's presenter and 'relationship expert' establish the possibility of confrontation. *Aftermath* invites the original participants to re-engage with each other, to unravel and unpick the reconciliation that has occurred in the programme itself. In this way, *Aftermath* constructs viewers out of the participants and sets up another revelation – now, like us as viewers, they can see what *really* happened. The programme pays particular attention to the wife's reactions and the family generally supports her views, reiterating her position as the superior wife. Unlike the original format, this follow-on programme does not neatly resolve the issues between the couples and often ends with the trite suggestion that people are just different.

Emotional excess is figured through this extension of the programme as something that can teach both its participants and viewers something. As in melodrama, excess is understood as potentially disruptive and as a potential to emphasise the emotional content. It is also a site of emotional identification with the audience. Viewers might find themselves saying, 'I'm not like that', or, conversely, hear their partners saying, 'You're just like that.' As Hill points out: 'To say "I'm not like that" implies a strong recognition of certain character traits and values that are perceived as external to the self' (2007: 202). Far from teaching the viewer or participant something, the programme perpetuates an individualised response and this is what shuts down any real potential for social change.

Emotional engagements

In presenting some of these ideas at a symposium on emotion and affect,[1] I was told by several respondents that although they were aware of the critical aspects of lifestyle programming I discussed, they admitted that they often found themselves emotionally moved by these shows. So, although I have argued for the ways in which we must think critically about the use of emotion in reality and lifestyle programmes, I am also aware that many viewers do gain something from these texts and enjoy watching them (and even become 'hooked'). Many viewers find themselves crying during lifestyle or reality television despite their critical opinions of the programme. I want to suggest that two things are important within this consideration of the use of emotion in reality and lifestyle television: first, it is important to point out that although viewers can be critical of these texts they also find themselves emotionally moved by them. Secondly, it is necessary to think about how feelings and emotions are manipulated within these programmes. In other words, we need also to consider the 'ugly feelings' that are produced in these texts and the effect or consequences they have on viewers.

Work on emotions often produces ambivalent feelings. On the one hand, as I have suggested, it is possible to be critical of the use of emotion in the text, and yet, on the other, people often find themselves responding to these texts emotionally. As I have argued elsewhere, the value of emotion in a text can be understood as something that creates good television and constructs a sense of connectedness and belonging (Gorton 2006).

Although most viewers have learned through their television-watching experience to be critical of what they watch, they may also find themselves emotionally involved with the characters or participants. This establishes an uneasy relationship for the viewer between their emotional reactions and their critical judgements. They might believe reality programmes to be rubbish but find themselves tuning in each night and getting emotionally involved.

It is an uneasy relationship that can be likened to that between feminism and the beauty industry. In 'Discipline and pleasure: the uneasy relationship between feminism and the beauty industry' (2006), for instance, Paula Black discusses the way women participate in the beauty industry even though they are aware of the way they are being positioned as 'dupes'. In other words, even though some women are aware of the 'trap' of this industry, they participate either because they take pleasure in the experience or because they feel that they must keep up with beauty regimes in order to participate in a world that demands such perfection. Despite their critical awareness and ability to recognise the role they are playing within such an industry, many women find pleasure in manicures, massages and in the possibility that these treatments will make them look more beautiful, even while aware that 'beauty' is a constructed ideology. Likewise, I would argue, there are many viewers who take pleasure in reality and lifestyle programmes even when they are conscious of their constructed and ideologically questionable nature. My students, for instance, often tell me that although they know many reality programmes, such as *Big Brother* or *American Idol* (Fremantle Media, 2002–), are heavily edited, they take pleasure in watching them and even find themselves crying during the back stories. This is not to say that all viewers respond to this kind of double-thinking, but to underline that even those aware of the constructed nature of these programmes still enjoy their viewing experience: their critical knowledge does not always mediate against their viewing pleasures.

A paradox emerges here and runs throughout reality and lifestyle programming. One the one hand, we, as viewers, are drawn into the emotional situations the characters find themselves in and yet, on the other hand, we are also encouraged to speculate, judge and attend to the choices and decisions the families have made and continue to make. Helen Piper suggests that 'there is clearly an affective invitation [in *Wife Swap*] to identify with the women's feelings and responses, but there is also an invitation to judge according to subjective concepts of "normal" (and by implication abnormal) domestic arrangements' (2004: 276). This dual-response of empathising and judging confuses easy lines of identification with the participants. As Piper points out: 'you might share Ann's distaste of Diane's family's reliance on deep-fried food, for example, but does that oblige you to identify with her other lower-middle-class pretensions?' (2004: 279). However, instead of understanding the relationship between viewers and participants as Piper outlines, we can instead suggest that this confusion of empathy and judgement means that viewers are selecting and choosing what aspects of both wives s/he feels are acceptable, and this perhaps means that viewers are actively participating in the act of "choosing, changing and transforming'.

Berlant refers to the 'paradox of partial legibility' in her work on public intimacy and suggests that 'the experience of social hierarchy is intensely individuating, yet it also makes people public and generic: it turns them into *kinds* of people who are both attached to and underdescribed by the identities that organise them' (1997: 1). As I suggested earlier, *Wife Swap* is about differing wifely roles – what *kind* of wife a wife can be. The focus on the *kind* of wife rather than who the wife herself is means that we, as viewers, only partially attach ourselves to these people; the lack of description allows us to enter in our own judgements and choices.

'Ugly feelings'

This is perhaps the 'ugly' side of reality and lifestyle programmes – the notion that many viewers watch these programmes to feel better about themselves (at the expense of others). If we return to the revelation side of reality and lifestyle programmes we can appreciate that they incorporate a certain sense of anxiety within their structure. Anxiety, as Sianne Ngai points out in *Ugly Feelings*, is an 'expectant emotion' (along with fear and hope) (2005). Viewers expect to feel certain emotions when watching reality and lifestyle programmes, even if one of those emotions is boredom. They might also feel contempt and disgust, whether this is figured in terms of class or morality. Indeed, one of the most common responses among the wives on *Wife Swap* is contempt: often one wife feels that she does things much better and takes a moral position against her 'other'. In countless instances the wives are filmed crying, getting angry or shouting about the practices of their counterpart. This establishes permission on the part of the viewer to enter in her opinions and judgements. It allows the viewer to take sides or to 'rise above' the quarrelling women and feel superior to both. Indeed, the viewer, who is allowed to see the actions of both wives, is placed in a judgemental position – empowered to choose which wife, if any, is 'right'.

Ngai argues that the 'logic of "anxiety" and that of "projection," as a form of spatial displacement, converge in the production of a distinct kind of knowledge-seeking subject' (2005: 215). Anxiety, Ngai contends, 'emerges as a form of dispositioning that paradoxically relocates, reorients, or repositions the subject thrown – performing an "individualization" (as Heidegger puts it) that restores and ultimately validates the trajectory of the analyzing subject's inquiry' (2005: 247). Following Ngai's analysis, it is possible to understand the viewer of reality and lifestyle programmes as someone who discovers a sense of validation through the projection of emotion onto her screen counterparts. The viewer is able to displace her own anxieties onto the screen character and feel a sense of validation in knowing that 'she' (the individual) is 'right'.

Jane Shattuc's article entitled 'having a good cry over *The Color Purple*' (1994) is important to this chapter as it draws attention to feminism's failure to resolve the 'affective power of the melodramatic text' (1994: 147); and ultimately this is what we are dealing with in *Wife Swap* – the problem of solving the tension that is produced by such an affective text (i.e. do we cry, laugh or look on in disgust?). Shattuc suggests that a dual hermeneutic is at work in these texts: 'a positive hermeneutic of the "good cry" which recuperates the Utopian moment, the authentic kernel, from which they draw their emotional power, and a negative hermeneutic that discloses their complicity with white patriarchal ideology' (1994: 152). Perhaps Shattuc's model is one way for us to see what happens in a programme such as *Wife Swap*. As viewers we are drawn into an emotional engagement with the participants which on many levels reiterates our feelings of community, belonging and humanity; and yet we are also complicit in perpetuating an individualised society that encourages us to 'choose, change and transform' and to judge those who do it badly.

Note

1. Thanks to the participants of the 'Emotion, affect, culture: feminist engagements', symposium at Goldsmiths College, University of London, June 2006.

Discussion/Exercises

1. Discuss ways in which programmes fashion emotion and draw their viewers into a moral judgement about the participants and their lifestyle choices. Is this fashioning of emotion specific to lifestyle and reality programming, or do you see it operating in other television genres?
2. Drawing on one programme in particular, closely analyse the way in which emotion is used to engage viewers.

Further reading

Bauman, Zygmunt (2001), *The Individualized Society*, Cambridge: Polity Press.

Beck, Ulrich and Elisabeth Beck-Gernsheim (2001), *Individualisation: Institutionalized Individualism and Its Social and Political Consequences*, Cambridge: Polity Press.

Biressi, Anita and Heather Nunn (2004), *Reality TV: Realism and Revelation*, London: Wallflower Press.

Black, Paula (2006), 'Discipline and pleasure: the uneasy relationship between feminism and the beauty industry', in J. Hollows and R. Moseley (eds), *Feminism in Popular Culture*, Oxford: Berg, pp. 143–59.

Brunsdon, Charlotte (2004), 'Lifestyling Britain: the 8–9 Slot on British television', in Lynn Spigel and Jan Olsson (eds), *Television after TV: Essays on a Medium in Transition*, Durham, NC: Duke University Press, pp. 75–92.

Fairclough, Kirsty (2004), 'Women's work? *Wife Swap* and the reality problem', *Feminist Media Studies*, 4(3): 344–6.

Giddens, Anthony (1990), *The Consequences of Modernity*, Cambridge: Polity Press.

Giddens, Anthony (1991), *Modernity and Self-Identity*, Cambridge: Polity Press.

Morley, David (2000), *Home Territories: Media, Mobility and Identity*, London and New York: Routledge.

Moseley, Rachel (2000), 'Makeover takeover on British television', *Screen*, 41(3): 299–314.

Piper, Helen (2004), 'Reality TV, *Wife Swap* and the drama of banality', *Screen*, 45(4): 273–86.

Shattuc, Jane (1994), 'Having a good cry over *The Colour Purple*: the problem of affect and imperialism in feminist theory', in J. Bratton, C. Gledhill and J. Cook (eds), *Melodrama: Stage Picture Screen*, London: British Film Institute, pp. 147–56.

Wood, Helen and Beverley Skeggs (2004), 'Notes on ethical scenarios of self on british reality TV', *Feminist Media Studies*, 4(2): 205–7.

8 Emotional Rescue: *The Sopranos* (HBO 1999–2007), *ER* (NBC 1994–) and *State of Play* (BBC1 2003)

This chapter will continue to draw on the theoretical work presented in the first half of the book in order to examine how emotion is constructed in what Robin Nelson refers to as 'contemporary high-end TV drama' (2007). As discussed in Chapter 5, he argues that there is a '"look" and "feel" of the aesthetics of much "high-end" contemporary television' (2007: 19) that has demanded new attention to television aesthetics. This demand for an aesthetic criteria in television studies, articulated by Charlotte Brunsdon in 1990 and pursued by John Thornton Caldwell in *Televisuality* (1995), has been taken up recently by television academics, such as Jason Jacobs (2000, 2006), Sarah Cardwell (2005, 2006), Karen Lury (2005) and Greg M. Smith (2007). In her excellent work on 'television aesthetics', for instance, Sarah Cardwell demonstrates the importance of a close analysis in television studies through her attention to Stephen Poliakoff's *Perfect Strangers* (2001). Concentrating on specific scenes enables Cardwell to comment on the way Poliakoff's work engages the viewer emotionally. She argues that: 'rather than a determined movement towards a moment of intense emotion, there is a continual "pulling back" from a clearly defined emotional release' (Cardwell 2005: 184). Cardwell reaches this conclusion through her close analysis of Poliakoff's work and through her engagement with cognitive film theory, namely, through Smith's notion of 'mood-cues' and 'emotional markers' (see Chapter 5). She argues that the sequence in Poliakoff's work that she identifies 'avoids the emotion markers that would ordinarily be considered vital to the maintenance of mood' (2005: 184). Cardwell also focuses particular attention on image and montage, music, dialogue and sound, and the 'pleasures of repetition' that she sees as distinctive to Poliakoff's work. Her work demonstrates a way of not only valuing the aesthetics of television but also of 'pithing' (Carroll) the emotional structure of the text. Indeed, her attention to the specificities of the text and her attention to what the text does open up new ways of appreciating television.

In *Beautiful TV: The Art and Argument of Ally McBeal*, Greg M. Smith takes the attention to the formal qualities of a text to a new level by devoting an entire book to one series. Smith convincingly argues for the importance of developing formal and narrative tools to discuss a five-season television series such as *Ally McBeal* and his work justifies the need to analyse a television text in its entirety (2007: 12). Although a close analysis of this kind is not possible within the scope of this book, this chapter focuses on specific formal qualities within 'quality' television series in order to demonstrate the way emotion is constructed and valued.

Emotional rescue

The American television series, *ER*, which has been running since 1994, offers a pertinent example in considering how emotion is constructed on television. The hospital drama follows the lives of doctors and nurses as they attempt to save lives in the Emergency Room of a Chicago hospital. As a series, the programme has received numerous accolades for its dramatic plot lines and characters. The original cast, starring Anthony Edwards, George Clooney, Laura Innes, Eriq La Salle, Noah Wyle and Juliana Margulies illustrated that television could deliver strong performances and offer something almost as good as film. Although very few of the original cast remain, the new cast continues the tradition of strong acting and performance and the series as a whole continues to deliver 'high-end' drama and is a long-time staple of 'must-see TV' in the US and the UK.

I want to focus in particular on an episode in Season One entitled 'Love's Labours Lost'. The episode drew critical attention and won Emmy Awards for Writing, Directing, Editing and Sound Mixing. It begins with Dr Mark Greene (Anthony Edwards) and Dr Doug Ross (George Clooney) playing a game of football in the street outside the hospital's back entrance. Mark notices a car speeding towards Doug and draws his attention just in time for him to move out of the way. A body is thrown out of the door and tumbles onto the street. The two doctors act immediately and the camera follows as they take the man into the operating room. The opening sequence establishes a sense of unease for the viewer. Lulled into the ordinary shot of two men playing ball, the viewer does not anticipate any danger. The fact that Ross moves away just in time heightens the viewer's awareness that lives are at stake.

One of the defining features of *ER* is the clever banter between its central characters. It often serves as light relief between scenes of dramatic life-saving. The banter also establishes a connection between the characters: as viewers we have the sense that they are a 'team' – that they are bound together by the job they perform. Glances across the operating table also serve to underline an unspoken understanding that runs through them – it distinguishes them from their patients and from senior doctors or management.

The central story in 'Love's Labours Lost' involves a young, pregnant couple, Sean and Jodi O'Brien (Bradley Whitford and Colleen Flynn). They have come to the *ER* because Jodi has been going to the toilet 'every 30 seconds'. Their visit is framed as routine and the couple are characterised as nice, happy and good-natured people. To the more experienced viewer of the series, this immediately suggests that all will not be as straightforward as it seems. And sure enough, moments after they leave, the man runs back into the ER hysterically demanding that someone attend to his wife, who has fallen unconscious in the car.

The episode features a digital clock in the right-hand corner of the screen. We, as viewers, are always aware of the way time is passing and begin to link this to the rapid deterioration of Jodi's condition. The clock, rarely used in *ER* episodes (and before *24* was in production), also reminds the viewers how long Mark is involved with this patient and constructs a sense of empathy both with Mark and with the patient. Throughout the first half of the episode, Mark believes he can handle the delivery of her baby and is seen as very secure and self-confident. As if to punish him for his pride, he slowly loses control of the situation and the patient: she dies on the operating table, following an emergency caesarean.

Editing is crucial to establishing emotion in *ER*. The fast pace builds tension and develops what Warhol, discussed in Chapter 6, refers to in soap operas as an 'undertow' of emotion (2003: 119). Although *ER* is not aired daily like soaps (except in the case of reruns) viewers are similarly led along a 'wave of feeling' until the climax, usually occurring three-quarters of the way through the episode. At this point, the tension, largely constructed through the tight editing, slows down and encourages viewers to release emotion. The final segment of the episode often offers a resolution and time to reflect on the feelings established throughout the episode. The ending might also anticipate the drama for the following week and indeed all the episodes, like soaps, embed different story arcs that reach their climax later on in the series. However, in a drama such as *ER*, viewers are not expected to know the characters as intimately as a programme such as *The Sopranos* (as will be discussed later in this chapter). Indeed, the featuring of minor characters, ones that will be 'in hospital' for from one to three episodes, means that as viewers we are used to getting close to characters for a brief period of time.

Throughout 'Love's Labours Lost', music is used to heighten the sense of anxiety and or loss that pervades the episode. In its final sequence, Mark is shown walking through hospital doors: the only sound we can hear is the doors opening and shutting. The camera pans to a room where Mr O'Brien holds his newborn son in a rocking chair. He is looking at his son, which gives Mark time to look at him before he catches his attention. The camera closes in as Mark enters the room and tells Mr O'Brien something. There is no sound, so we do not know what he says, except that we know he has told him his wife is dead because he suddenly starts to weep. The fact that there is no sound and that we cannot hear the words that are chosen or the response made heightens a viewer's experience of emotion. The silence or 'white space' allows us to enter in our own dialogue. The words Mark tells Mr O'Brien are words no one ever wants to hear about a beloved and so the silence works on many different levels. The ending, although joyful because the child survives, is also filled with loss, and awareness that the series will not always deliver happy endings.

ER, now in its final series, provides long-time viewers with a chance to become emotionally involved in the storylines of its characters and even makes reference to the long 'history' of affective lives that have developed. For instance, Chuny (Laura Cerón), one of the longest-running characters in the series, says that she 'remembers when Doug Ross and Mark Greene ran the place, to which Sam, one of the newer cast members says, 'Who?' The moment is very brief but it is there to speak to the long-time fans of the show and to remind viewers of the intimate history of the programme itself. Indeed the episode to which I am referring, 'The Blackout', focuses on Abi's (Maura Tierney) breakdown and one-night stand with her new supervisor while Luca (Goran Visnjic), her husband, is in Croatia. Those who are long-time watchers of *ER* know about not only Abi's alcoholism but also her family's history of mental illness. This knowledge brings added emotional engagement to watching this character's breakdown, but for someone who has never seen the series it does not preclude an emotional attachment to the piece. Part of what this demonstrates is television's increasing hybridity: the soap formula is visible in many dramas such as *The Sopranos* and *ER* and the embededness of fan relations is also evident – but the emotional engagement remains forefront and one of the sure ways to develop new viewers/fans. It also suggests the way in which television, unlike film, must construct itself for faithful *and* casual viewers. Unlike film, television needs to be more available to a wider audience and therefore the emotional dimension may not always be as thought-provoking or moving as film.

Emotional strands

In his lecture to the Royal Television Society (2005), discussed in Chapter 6, British television writer Paul Abbott explains that he wrote the 'emotional strands' for *State of Play* (2003) before doing the research on politics and journalism. He also points out that he learned to use the 'white space' to 'give the audience a job to do in pinning the story down'. He explains that he 'mentally removed every second scene: Skip the explanatory pages and dive onto the next story beat'. Abbott argues that:

> What's not said communicates more dignity and humanity and complexity than any line of dialogue could ever transmit. Films have done this for years. We love films for being able to do this. But over and over again, t.v. insists on filling the white space with ink.

Not only does the 'white space' communicate dignity and humanity, it constructs emotion, and *State of Play* is an excellent example of this.

State of Play (n.d.) is in production at the time of writing as a movie, starring Ben Affleck, Russell Crowe and Helen Mirren, which further demonstrates the links between 'quality' television and film. Nelson describes *State of Play* as: 'a consummate political thriller, sustaining something of the political critique associated with the British social realist tradition but produced with a multi-layered narrative complexity and contemporary visual stylishness' (2007: 201). Abbott's work follows in a tradition of 'serious' British drama. *Cathy Come Home* (BBC 1966), *Boys from the Blackstuff* (BBC 1982) and *One Summer* (YTV 1983) influenced subsequent generations to pay close attention to the writing in terms of emotional development. Abbott, who set up a teatime drama with Kay Mellor called *Children's Ward* (ITV 1998–2000), takes a similar approach to his work. Series such as *Clocking Off* (BBC 2000–3) and *Shameless* (Channel 4 2004–) illustrate his ability to move his audiences emotionally, which is something, as discussed in the last chapter, that he values.

State of Play, starring John Simm and David Morrissey, begins with the murder of a young black boy and a twenty-something woman who is a researcher for an up-and-coming political figure. In the press conference announcing her death, Stephen Collins (David Morrissey) becomes very emotional and this leads to a media frenzy speculating on their relationship. The series is fast paced and filled with emotional explosions: similar to *ER*, music, editing and acting work together to create an emotionally engaging text. Nelson does an admirable job of taking his reader through the opening episode of *State of Play* (2007: 201–11), so I do not want to duplicate this work, rather I would stress, as does Nelson, the way in which Abbott loads each episode with clues and teasers that keep the audience hooked in for more. But these hooks are not simply tied to the whodunit plot, rather they set up a complex emotional backdrop for the rest of the series. Viewers are invited into the world Abbott has constructed and taken on an emotional journey filled with highs and lows – he strands the piece very carefully, intricately weaving in different relationships and sub-plots. This process of stranding can be attributed to most dramas, so it is not to argue that *State of Play* offers a unique example; instead, what I am arguing is that a programme such as *State of Play* illustrates stranding at its best and most emotionally evocative.

Part of this comes from the two-stranded narrative embedded in Stephen Collins's character. At the beginning of the series we are offered one version of Stephen: that of a promising political figure caught in an illicit affair with his researcher. As the series develops, so does our understanding of Collins's character, and this is facilitated throughout by his relationship with Cal. As viewers we are aligned with Cal, who is both a friend to Stephen and someone interested in uncovering the 'truth' of the murders that open the series. When we discover that Stephen is not simply complicit in having an affair, which many viewers are likely to forgive, but also involved with a complex scheme involving oil companies, our ability to judge characters is undermined. Collins's character has not changed but our relationship to him alters dramatically once we begin to see the whole picture. In this way, Abbott starts with a small detail and fleshes it out until a broad landscape emerges. In so doing, he constructs a narrative that continually disrupts interpretation, which forces the viewer to just go along for the ride.

Learning to love the mafia

The Sopranos created by David Chase, finished its final season in 2007. The long-running series illustrates HBO's motto 'It's not TV, it's HBO' with its high-production value, acclaimed actors and emotive soundtrack. As Nelson argues: 'The very idea of a box office evokes a cinema visit rather than a domestic experience of the "goggle box" and, even allowing for the hype of HBO, there can be little doubt that visual style in television has become something to appreciated in itself, (2007: 112). Indeed, a recent collection entitled *It's Not TV: Watching*

HBO in the Post-Television Era (Leverette, Ott and Buckley 2008) illustrates the belief that HBO offers something distinct and unique in the televisual landscape.

The series follows the life of a New Jersey Crime family, the Sopranos. Anthony, 'Tony', who eventually becomes don of the family, suffers from panic attacks and sees a therapist, Dr Melfi, on a weekly basis. The series shares similarities in terms of plot to *Analyze This* (1999), starring Robert De Niro and Billy Crystal, but goes beyond this in terms of the emotional involvement established through strong characters such as 'Tony' (James Gandolfini) and his wife, Carmela (Edie Falco). *The Sopranos* has been the subject of numerous academic and non-academic books, including: *The Psychology of The Sopranos: Love, Death, Desire and Betrayal in America's Favorite Gangster Family* (2002), by Glen O. Gabbard; *This Thing of Ours* (2002), edited by David Lavery; *The Sopranos and Philosophy: I Kill Therefore I Am* (2004), by Richard Greene and Peter Vernezze; *The Sopranos on the Couch: Analyzing Television's Greatest Series* (2003), by Maurice Yacowar; *A Sitdown with the Sopranos: Watching Italian American Culture on TV's Most Talked-About Series* (2002), edited by Regina Barreca; and *Reading The Sopranos* (2006), edited by David Lavery, and, as Lavery points out, *Sopranos* is the subject of over fifty individual essays in journals such as *The Journal of Popular Film and Television, The Journal of Popular Culture* and *Film Quarterly* (2006: 7). In his work on 'high-end' drama, Nelson refers to *The Sopranos* as 'a generic hybrid of the mafia gangster movie genre with psychological drama and soap' (2007: 27), while Creeber, in *Serial Television* (2004), argues that '*The Sopranos* reminds us of the power of television genre to continually reinvent itself, revealing its tendency not only to repeat and rehash the old, but also its unique ability to occasionally create a new dramatic universe altogether' (2004: 108).

Interest in *The Sopranos* within television studies demonstrates Bird's assertion that television series enjoyed by academics are often the subject of academic research. However, it is not simply for its enjoyment value that I refer to this series as an example. I have chosen to focus on *The Sopranos* because, unlike the other series discussed in this chapter, emotion is slowly developed and depends on characterisation to a greater extent than the others. As Nelson points out:

> over time, regular viewers can build up a sense of an intimate knowledge of Tony and Carmela Soprano as their marriage comes under strain . . . such that there is a strong, close-up, continuing serial dimension to viewing, offering a version of the pleasures of soap intimacy. (2007: 29–30)

It is to this slow-building intimacy that I want to turn by focusing in particular on 'Carmela'.

Carmela Soprano holds a unique position as wife to the boss of the family. One of the dominant narratives in Season Four is Carmela's attempt to secure her family's financial future, fearing her husband might be killed. She begins by asking Tony to meet with her cousin, who is a financial advisor, and succeeds in having him agree to some stock portfolios, but he refuses to sign a life policy, having been advised by his accountant that this ties him in completely to his wife. Soon she realises that Tony has seduced her cousin into his inner circle, so she no longer has any control over his suggestions. Taking matters into her own hands, she loots the cash Tony has stored in the garden and invests the money in four different investment firms. Although Tony discovers the missing cash he also finds a fingernail tip, of one of his lovers, which Carmela has placed with his wallet and keys. In so doing, she prevents him from raising the issue of the missing cash and secures her financial future.

This is just a brief snapshot of the kind of female empowerment offered in *The Sopranos*. It is an agency firmly rooted in the domestic and therefore with its limitations, all of which are explicitly dealt with in the narrative. But it is a kind of agency that many women can relate to and even enjoy. Indeed, in her work on 'melodramatic identification' Ien Ang suggests that: '[f]antasy and fiction then, are the safe spaces of excess in the interstices of ordered social life where one has to keep oneself strategically under control' (1997: 164). In the fantasy world of *The Sopranos*, Carmela provides some viewers with a sense that enough cooking, resourceful thinking and clever innuendos can get a woman, with relatively little power, whatever she wants. It gives these traditional sites of femininity new power and allows a viewer the fantasy that they can make a difference with limited resources.

But there is something more here. Carmela continually questions her role as first wife of the Mafia family. At times she wants to close her eyes to the part she plays in the family dynamic and yet, at other times, she uses her 'family' connections to get what she wants for her children or herself. In *The Psychology of The Sopranos* (2002), Glen Gabbard argues that, like Tony's mother, Livia, Carmela often emotionally manipulates Tony to get what she wants (2002: 129). However, this analysis seems too one dimensional – the series is not only about Carmela manipulating Tony but also about the emotional dilemmas Carmela experiences being Tony's wife. In 'Second Opinion' (Season Three, Episode 7), for instance, Carmela is forced to confront her own participation in the Mafia and begins to question whether or not she should stay with Tony.

Following Salvatore's (Big Pussy) (Vincent Pastore) death, Tony is too busy dealing with nightmares about talking fish, Uncle Junior's (Dominic Chianese) cancer and problems between Christopher (Michael Imperioli) and Paulie (Tony Sirico) to recognise Carmela's 'empty-nest' syndrome and increasing doubts over whether she should be with a man like Tony. Her mother tells her: 'The man's got two speeds: moping and screaming – when he's here', which underlines her disappointment in Carmela's choice of husband. When Carmela reminds her parents of the advantages Tony brings them, her mother sarcastically replies: 'The waters don't part for you wherever you go?' To which Carmela responds: 'I earn it, you two get a free pass', reflecting Carmela's awareness of her complicity and role vis à vie the Mafia. The notion that Carmela 'earns' her keep is reiterated later in the episode when Carmela visits her daughter Meadow (Jamie-Lynn Sigler) before her meeting with the university dean to discuss 'development' (i.e. donating money to Columbia to ensure Meadow's success). Annoyed that Carmela will not accept that Tony was the reason for her latest break-up, Meadow tells her, 'Look, don't drag me into whatever bullshit accommodational pretence you've got worked out with Daddy', to which Carmela replies, What? Was that last night's reading assignment?' The dialogue between them, typical of the strength of writing on *The Sopranos*, reflects the way in which Carmela and Meadow are growing apart intellectually and yet also reveals the intimacy between them and the acceptance that being part of a Mafia family involves more pretence than others.

After meeting privately with Dr Melfi, Carmela decides to see her own therapist, one Dr Melfi recommends, a former teacher, Dr Krakower (Sully Boyle). During their session Carmela reveals that her husband works for organised crime. Dr Krakower says, 'the Mafia' – words that cause Carmela to visibly shake, exclaim, 'Oh Jesus', and then respond, 'So what?' Her confusion, rejection, fear and denial are palpable and we, as viewers, can see the internal struggle she confronts daily. Dr Krakower, however, sees things less sympathetically. He tells her that he will not accept her blood money and that she should leave Tony and take the children; he ends the session by telling her, 'One thing you can never say is that you haven't been told', to which she meekly replies, 'I see, you're right, I see.' The episode ends with Carmela on the couch, this time in the family home, with Tony sitting across from her, which in many ways replicates the scenes of analysis shown earlier in the episode (in Dr Melfi's office and later in Dr Krakower's office). Importantly, however, in this analytic scene, Carmela has her body turned completely away from Tony and delivers all her lines without looking at him, including her admission that she agreed to pay Columbia the $50,000 they wanted. When he reminds her that he only wanted to pay $5,000, she turns her head, looks him in the eyes and tells him, 'You gotta do something nice for me today. This is what I want.' And that is exactly what she gets. Gabbard's suggestion that Carmela emotionally manipulates Tony is true insofar as she gets what she wants, primarily for her children, but it is not without costs to her emotionally and bears little resemblance to the emotional beating Tony's mother gives him.[1]

Why might viewers be drawn to Carmela? I would argue that one answer lies in the serial structure of programmes such as *The Sopranos*. Whether you watch the show week by week or two episodes at a time on DVD, a viewer is allowed and even encouraged to enter the fictional world of the Sopranos and follow them through their own struggles, happiness, tragedies etc. Over six seasons, I have witnessed Carmela's emotional journey as wife, mother and woman which at various times and in various ways has affected my own experiences. Watching other people's fictional lives unfold on screen gives a viewer a chance to reflect, to experience things vicariously, to talk to a partner (who might be watching too) and enter into conversations about your own domestic arrangements. In other words, it opens up a space which inevitably allows us to think differently about gender and identity. The longevity of a series and its ability to construct an intimate world is distinct from the experience one might have watching a film. No matter how adept a film is at constructing an intimate portrayal of a person's life, it does not compare with the slow-building portrait offered in a long-running series on television. The everydayness of television allows viewers to witness the ambivalence, contradiction and confusion that bound most of our lives.

In their chapter on Carmela and the post-feminist dilemma, Janet McCabe and Kim Akass thoughtfully attempt to work through Carmela's appeal to viewers, despite her rejection of many feminist values. Carmela does not imagine herself as a feminist, indeed she tells her close friend 'Rosalie Aprille' that she is not a feminist but wants to have an equal relationship with her husband when it comes to the financial stability of their family. She tells Roe, 'I'm no feminist. I'm not saying 50/50. But Jeez' ('Mergers and Acquisitions' 4:8). McCabe and Akass admit that they find writing about their enjoyment of a character like Carmela very difficult. They find that there is lack of discourse available within feminist theory to talk about the everyday lives of women. They argue:

> But women like Carmela – no feminist, slipping through the cracks of feminism, not quite making the theoretical cut, representing a

dominance many of us find hard to reconcile ourselves with – have much to tell us about our continued investment in approved hetero-sexual scripts, deals that must be struck, often working with tools that many of us find deplorable, and the contradictions we live with. Carmela's complex dilemmas are ours. She may not be a feminist, but what she represents reveals the limits of what can and cannot be said. In her resistance she holds out the promise of change. (2006: 55)

Their point is very well articulated given the complex and difficult nature of an emotional engagement with a character like Carmela. What they suggest is not only the need for more feminist theory that engages with the everyday but also theory that can begin to handle the emotional involvement in characters such as Carmela, who appeal to viewers even though they might not share the characters' moral, ethical, political beliefs. Ang, as I have pointed out, has gone some way towards theorising this – her research revealed that women enjoyed a morally 'bad' character like Sue Ellen from *Dallas* because she offered vicarious pleasures. But a character like Carmela is more complex than Sue Ellen. She struggles with the choices she makes and takes her viewers along with her. Her ambivalence and contradictions are central to her characterisation and central to the enjoyment viewers experience because they can reflect the paradoxical relationship many women have to family life, to feminism and to 'having it all'.

Smith persuasively argues that 'what *Ally McBeal* demonstrates is that a serial can progress by changing its basic attitude toward the characters, by asking the audience to re-evaluate its judgments of characters' behav-iours, not by changing the characters themselves' (2007: 74). Smith's contention holds true for *The Sopranos* in that the audience is compelled to continually re-evaluate their feelings towards Tony and Carmela, and the rest of the ensemble cast. Carmela's character is perhaps most com-pelling in terms of Smith's argument because she vacillates between accepting her position within the Mafia and actively rejecting it. Her character's complexity and emotional vulnerability invite us in and chal-lenge us to reconsider our relationship to morality, ethics and marriage.

Conclusion

All of the programmes discussed in this chapter achieve an emotional response from their audience through their attention to qualities such as characterisation, narrative, editing, music and acting. I have argued that *The Sopranos* offers an example of how intimacy is developed over the series through a focus on Carmela. Of course this is not limited to

The Sopranos, and series such as *ER* illustrate how a long-running series develops a sense of familiarity for viewers. What these three examples of 'quality' television illustrate is the importance of strong, contradictory characters to an emotional engagement with their audiences.

Note

1. The scene between Carmela and Dr Krakower is a pivotal one and has been discussed by other critics such as Gabbard and McCabe and Akass. Gabbard suggests, for instance, that: 'Carmel's encounter with Dr Krakower makes it clear she is not simply a victim' (2002: 133); while McCabe and Akass suggest that her visit to Dr Krakower demonstrates that: 'Carmela is committed to working with contradiction and inconsistency in order to collude "with approved scripts" (Heywood and Drake 1997: 14)' (2006: 48).

Web reference

The Huw Wheldon Lecture with Paul Abbott, Royal Television Society (2005) http://www.rts.org.uk/Information_page_+_3_pic_det.asp?id=4282&sec_id=652

Exercises

1. Watch an episode of 'high-end' television drama, such as the work discussed in this chapter. After viewing the episode, write down what qualities of the text you feel elicit emotion from their viewers. Consider the theoretical work discussed in Chapters 4 and 5. Do you feel that cognitive film theory helps us to think through emotion in television?

2. In *Beautiful TV* (2007) Smith argues for the importance of watching a series in its entirety (12); Choose a serial narrative such as *Ally McBeal*, *Clocking Off* or *The Street* and watch the entire text. As Smith points out, 'the formal and narrative tools developed to discuss a 90-minute feature film need to be adapted to look at a 111-hour narrative such as *Ally McBeal*, (2007: 12). Critically discuss ways in which this adaptation is possible.

3. Consider writing and/or directing an episode of *ER*, *State of Play* or *The Sopranos*. Or think about how you would perform one of the character roles. What aspects would you have to pay attention to in order to achieve the style, look and feel of the series? Which character do you find most emotionally engaging? Why?

Further reading

Cardwell, Sarah (2005), '"Television aesthetics" and close analysis: style, mood and engagement in *Perfect Strangers* (Stephen Poliakoff, 2001)', in John Gibbs and Douglas Pye (eds), *Style and Meaning: Studies in the Detailed Analysis of Film*, Manchester: Manchester University Press, pp. 179–94.

Jacobs, Jason (2000), *The Intimate Screen: Early British Television Drama*, Oxford: Oxford University Press.

Leverette, Marc, Brian L. Ott and Cara Louise Buckley (eds) (2008), *It's Not TV: Watching HBO in the Post-Television Era*, New York and London: Routledge.

Lury, Karen (2005), *Interpreting Television*, London: Hodder Headline.

Nelson, Robin (2007), *State of Play: Contemporary "High-End" TV Drama*, Manchester: Manchester University Press.

Smith, Greg M. (2007), *Beautiful TV: The Art and Argument of Ally McBeal*, Austin, TX: University of Texas Press.

9 Feminising Television: the Mother Role in *Six Feet Under* (HBO 2001–6) and *Brothers & Sisters* (ABC 2006–)

Following an analysis of three 'quality' television programmes, the last chapter considered formal qualities that elicit emotion, such as music, editing, characterisation, writing and the longevity of a series. This chapter focuses on one device in particular: it considers how the mother figure in two television series is used to draw out emotional and intimate details from the ensemble cast. In centring on the mother and her relationship to her children, the series foreground the affective attachments within families and the dramas that come from such close bonds. This chapter also considers the way in which feminism is raised, negotiated and handled in popular series such as *Six Feet Under* (HBO 2001–6) and *Brothers & Sisters* (ABC 2006–) in order to think about how the domestic, the 'home', frames and figures older women's sexuality.

Whether looking at television programmes such as *Sex and the City* (HBO 1998–2004), *Ally McBeal* (20th Century Fox 1997–2004) or films like *Bridget Jones's Diary* (Sharon Maguire 2001) from the position of their popularity, their presence within feminist theory or their appeal to viewers, theorists note the ambivalence and contradiction that mark them (see Lotz 2001; Arthurs 2004; Brunsdon 2006). One of the primary ways in which this contradiction and ambivalence is structured is through emotion. *Ally McBeal*, for instance, uses emotion to distinguish Ally's way of confronting problems in the workplace and in her life decisions. Her emotional responses, sometimes excessive ones, mark her ambivalence towards her career and lifestyle choices and reiterate her contradictory choices (see Gorton 2008a).

Women have traditionally been associated with emotion. As Probyn argues in her work on affect: 'That women have been associated with the emotions is so prevalent a notion in our culture that it can go unqualified' (2005: 81). Descriptions of films such as 'women's weepies' and 'chick flicks' reiterate the notion that to cry at movies is a gendered experience. And yet many men will admit to crying and finding themselves emotionally involved with what they watch. Critical work on romance fiction, such as Janice Radway's *Reading the Romance* (1984) or Tania Modleski's *Loving with a Vengeance* (1982) can be extended to think about the ways in which people prepare themselves for a good cry by watching particular programmes, whether a drama or a reality makeover programme.

Amanda D. Lotz and Sharon Marie Ross trace the origins of feminist television criticism to a combination of feminist film criticism, British cultural studies and feminist-led mass communication research (2004: 185). They argue that feminist television criticism grew out of a 'synthesis' of these and other intellectual influences. They also point towards the integral relationship between feminist theory and television studies: 'Feminist criticism and television studies were born together in [the 1970s], and while both struggled for a place in academic institutions, the youthfulness of television studies made it possible for feminist voices to emerge without having to overthrow an "old guard"' (2004: 186). It is significant that television studies developed at the same time as feminist criticism, and one consequence of this development is evident in the amount of work and engagement in television studies.

It is also significant that one of the most influential feminist television critics, Charlotte Brunsdon, points towards a 'feminisation' of television schedules in the 1990s (2000b: 169). Brunsdon argues that programmes typically scheduled for daytime viewing have moved into evening time slots; lifestyle television and its emphasis on the domestic began to dominate what Brunsdon refers to as the '8–9 slot' (2004). This has resulted in what Rachel Moseley identifies as a 'softening up of hard programming' and 'soaping' of television (2000: 301).[2] Soaps have historically featured 'strong' matriarchal roles and have much to do with 'mothers' and their relationships with their daughters (see Brunsdon 2000a: 11–12, 215). Part of what I am arguing here is that the prominence of the mother role in both *Six Feet Under* and *Brothers & Sisters* reflects the 'softening up' and 'soaping' of television that Moseley and Brunsdon identify.

Therefore, this chapter focuses on the domestic scene, constructions of intimacy, generations between mother and daughters and the mother figure within the context of both feminism and the feminisation of television. Drawing on the characters 'Ruth' (Frances Conroy) in HBO's *Six Feet Under* (2001–6) and 'Nora' (Sally Field) in ABC's *Brothers & Sisters* (2006–) as examples, the chapter argues that central to these representations is a dialogue with feminism – in each example there is an implicit struggle, often generational, that can be read as metaphoric of the ways in which contemporary popular culture continues to negotiate, frame and consider how feminism is relevant to women's lives. Part of this negotiation involves the emotional intimacy between the central characters and its resolution or deferral. More specifically, this intimacy is often framed through the relationship between mother and daughter. One of the implicit suggestions is that each generation must learn from the previous how to manage the balance between care and desire in the home and how to avoid letting home become the only way in which a woman is defined. In other words, the domestic takes on different meanings as it is passed through the generations. As Joanne Hollows argues, 'the meanings of the domestic, and domestic femininities, are contextual and historical and what operates as a site of subordination for some women may operate as the object of fantasy for others' (2006: 114). This chapter is concerned with how meanings of the domestic and of domestic femininities are negotiated through the body of the older woman in contemporary television. I shall argue that the mother figure in *Six Feet Under* and *Brothers & Sisters* is used as a device to validate the emphasis placed on emotion and intimacy within the series and leads in part to what Brunsdon identifies as the 'feminisation of television'.

In his discussion of aesthetics, Greg M. Smith draws on theoretical work by the Russian Formalists who were concerned with how 'devices' were used to realise particular 'functions' (2007: 9). The mother figure functions as a character that all other characters can open up to emotionally. She is seen as someone 'safe' to disclose feelings and share intimacies. These moments often happen between mother and daughter in the kitchen or bedroom. Whereas moments of emotional intensity shared between the other characters, particularly those contemporary to each other, are set in public domains. Perhaps the death of the patriarch and the rise of the matriarch in both series mark a reiteration of the significance of emotion and the feminine to its viewing public. But that is not all. The presence of emotional intimacy in these texts, centred on the mother figure, suggests that many viewers want this kind of emotional drama and that producers are fulfilling their demands. The move towards more emotional dramas reiterates the notion that television is becoming feminised.

Six Feet Under and the politics of experience

Each episode of *Six Feet Under* begins with an ending – of someone's life. The short vignette that opens each programme sets up the central themes of the series: death, loss, family and home. The final theme, home, is ever-present as both domestic home and funeral home are one; most of the characters either live or work within the home. The fact that their home is also a place of work and then, even further, a place where dead people are taken for display is certainly one that challenges some of the theorisations explored above. How do you feel a sense of calm and comfort in a home with a basement full of dead bodies? The series uses this fundamental discomfort to allow 'ghosts' to inhabit the place – on countless occasions the dead cadavers 'come to life' and converse with their caretakers, mostly about the problems the living are having but sometimes to say a final word about their own lives. Another recurring ghost is that of Nathaniel Fisher, Sr. who dies in the first episode of the series. The loss of the patriarch overshadows the home, literally, and also displaces some authority and responsibility onto his widow, Ruth, who steps into the position of matriarch, with much reluctance. Ruth is characterised as the ultimate domestic: hair swept into a bun, often wearing an apron, frequently at the kitchen table, the head of the family and the mother of most of the central characters in the programme. Over the five seasons viewers witnessed various changes in her persona: moments of revelation, honesty and fantasy, but her ability to care-take and be domestic is always emphasised. In this way, the figure of the older woman is defined by the entwining of her domestic duties and her emotional as well as physical care-taking, both of the living and of the dead.

In Season Five, Ruth's ability to look after all those she loves is challenged when her husband George has a relapse of depressive psychosis. Ruth joins a knitting circle in order to get out of the house but also to speak to others about her life. She is convinced by the women in the group to leave George. They suggest that she set him up in his own place and then go: that way, she has ensured that he is 'safe' within a domestic space but she no longer needs to be the one domesticating him. In the episode 'The rainbow of her reasons' (Season Five 2005), Ruth is temporarily removed from her responsibilities to George and allowed to enter the sacred circle of her sister's friends to celebrate the life of a deceased friend. The episode features a cameo appearance by Susie Bright, the author of, among other books, *Mommy's Little Girl* (2004), which offers a nod towards sexual freedom and exploration. What follows is something akin to a 'second wave' women's-only party around the kitchen table. The women celebrate the life of their friend, but, more importantly for Ruth, they envision a world where women are in control and men are only there for pleasure or childcare. Ruth literally lets her hair down and believes in the possibilities of this new female collective. The next day, as the women leave, Ruth asks one of them where they are meeting, fully believing that they are going to set up a commune as they fantasised the night before. When the woman smiles at her, she realises that she has mistaken drunken fantasies for real possibilities and she is faced with returning to the task of losing George. When she goes to see him, he has realised her plan and tells her that she is 'free'. The programme ends with Ruth in the hallway outside George's closed door. The episode plays with the dilemmas in women's liberation: Ruth is 'free' from her second husband, but what has this freedom cost and what does it offer her? Here the domestic is privileged as a nostalgic space for security and stability. And yet, the series as a whole constantly undermines the domestic – questioning and interrogating its permanence by undermining any real sense of security Ruth finds in the home.

Within feminist and cultural studies, as discussed in Chapter 4, there has been a renewed concern with understanding the role of emotions and affect in shaping individual and collective identities and in terms of rethinking the way in which the personal and political are framed. Lauren Berlant, for instance, in *The Queen of America Goes to Washington* (1997), argues that the feminist phrase 'the personal is the political' 'has now been reversed and redeployed on behalf of a staged crisis in the legitimacy of the most traditional, apolitical, sentimental patriarchal family values' (1997: 177–8). She goes on to suggest that the maxim today might be 'The political is the personal'. What Berlant argues is that instead of trying to validate the intimate and make it relevant in terms of the political, the political has become the personal, which means the individual is now responsible for making sure she is making the right decisions regarding life, love and death. Berlant later went on to make a wider point that the political public sphere is increasingly shifting to an intimate public sphere. What was once considered to be intimate is now splashed across the broadsheet headlines and offered up on reality television every night. She examines the way in which intimacy has increasingly been moved into the public domain and negotiated within contemporary culture. Perhaps one of the ways this comes through within television drama is through the figuring of the domestic and its relation to wider issues such as found in *Six Feet Under* regarding death, loss and home. Although operating very differently than found within reality television or talk show genres, there is still a sense that intimacy is at the forefront of the programme. However, the intimate is negotiated in a very different way, one that appears to be in more direct dialogue with feminist thinking and with the political. In fact, part of the success of *Six Feet Under* and its characterisation of 'Ruth' is that the programme avoids easy sentimentalism and resists legitimating traditional 'family values'.

As discussed previously, 'The rainbow of her reasons' begins with the death of Ruth's sister's close friend and focuses on the women who come to Ruth's home and who represent a 'second wave' sisterhood collective. The fact that Ruth fetishises the sense of belonging that this group engenders undermines the idea that simply being a mother and care-taker gives a woman purpose. One of the suggestions in the family values espoused by traditionalists is that a woman is not truly a woman until she is mother – that this experience of motherhood is what gives women a sense of connectedness and belonging. Ruth problematises this senti-mental idea insofar as she has a deep sense of regret at being *just* a mother and that her children, who are expected to provide this sense of purpose, are, in actuality, providing a sense of unbalance and frustration. Indeed, whenever Ruth does pursue her own desires, she is reminded that her position is that of mother rather than of lover. For Ruth, the moment of the women's collective seems to offer a way out of being alone in her position of responsibility within the home. The women talk over dinner and wine about sharing childcare, about a community without men and their incessant needs, and about working together. The dream of second wave feminism, or at least the perception of what that dream involved, is invoked, most acutely through Ruth's glassy-eyed gaze around the table. The next day, as Ruth prepares to go into the hills and set up their feminist collective, she is confronted by the reality that it was all longing and fantasy for a feminist life that never happened, not a true possibility. In this way, the episode reflects a kind of disappointment with feminism and, in particular, with second wave feminism. It also hints at a sense of superficiality – a suggestion that feminism is present in discourse and lyrics but not in action.

But there is more here, especially when we consider the episode in relation to the programme more broadly. This episode evokes an awak-ening in Ruth, a change in terms of her position within the world. And for me, this is very reflective of feminism and its continuing power. Although some women are disillusioned with feminism, representa-tions of feminist dilemmas continue to reflect upon and re-envision the position of women within contemporary culture. Feminist narratives continue to articulate the ways in which women come to understanding themselves and their place in the world. And this is demonstrated beau-tifully later on in the series when Brenda has given birth to her daughter Willa. Although very different kinds of women, and from different gen-erations, Ruth is able to support Brenda through her experience of single motherhood. Catching her on the stairs, a very domestic space, Ruth tells Brenda that she never really had any help from her husband in raising her children, that she was alone. Having just lost her husband,

Brenda is in the same position and, for once, is willing to accept Ruth's help. It is a very simple moment, and yet it holds the promise of a much more genuine kind of sisterhood than the idealised images offered in the episode described earlier. In this example, experience politicizes more effectively than theory insofar as it reunites a sense of collective struggle and initiates a deeper understanding between generations.

Brothers & Sisters and the trope of self-transformation

The consequences of intimacy are central to the storyline of *Brothers & Sisters*. Similar to *Six Feet Under*, the series begins with the death of the patriarch and the introduction to the ties that bind and suffocate an upper-middle-class family in California. Upon the death of William, his wife Nora (Sally Field) becomes the central figure in the family. However, her strength is soon undermined by the revelation that William not only embezzled money from the family business but also had a twenty-year affair with Holly (Patricia Wettig) which results in a daughter. One of the features of the series is the way in which any intimate secret (e.g. infidelity, marriage proposals or surprise parties) cannot be kept – the brothers and sisters quickly disseminate the truth across the family and its relations. The series proffers sentimental ideas about the nature of truth within family relationships yet troubles these notions at the same time.

'Nora' can be read in light of the seventies consciousness-raising novels. She has spent the majority of her life as a homemaker – caring for her five children and her husband until his death, which initiates a process of self-transformation. In seventies consciousness-raising novels such as Erica Jong's *Fear of Flying* ([1973] 1998) and Lisa Alther's *Kinflicks* ([1976] 1999) the narrative moves from the domestic and therefore oppressed to a constructed notion of liberation.[3] Imelda Whelehan notes that:

> The heroines of the [consciousness-raising] novels realize that there is something wrong in their lives and the plot of the novel often follows their quest to fix it . . . . The burden of the narrative turns on their analysis of these wrongs and the action they propose as a result – leaving the marital home . . . . determining to put their own aspirations first, and so on. (2005: 175)

Although Nora does not leave the home, she begins to pursue her own aspirations. However, they are often mediated by her inexperience and the needs of her children (which always take priority over her own). For instance, one of Nora's aspirations is to write and it is in her writing class that she meets Marc, her writing professor, whom she initially feels will liberate her. When he invites her over for a party, her friend convinces her that she should wear something seductive. She arrives dressed inappropriately for what turns out to be a dinner party for board members. One of them asks whether she is going to dance for them. This humiliating experience illustrates Nora's inadequacy outside the domestic scene.

Nora is explicitly contrasted with Holly, the woman with whom her husband had an affair, and to whom he confided his business plans. In the case of *Brothers & Sisters*, the women are divided between those who care and those who desire and Nora's place is firmly rooted in the former. When she attempts to join the family business and therefore compete with Holly she is shown to have little to no business knowledge or talent and eventually leaves to return to her place in the home. At the opening of her son Tommy's and Holly's joint wine venture, Holly seduces Nora's philandering boyfriend which results in a comical confrontation between the two women. Holly accuses Nora of having nothing more than 'a box full of recipes' whereas Nora indicts Holly for living off other people's money. They each vie over who William loved/desired more. Holly tells Nora, 'You should have seen the smile on his face when he came through the door', while Nora responds, 'Why did he always come home to me then? Even your own daughter would rather sleep at my house' (Season One, Episode 23, 'Grapes of wrath' 2007) . Here 'home' is figured as the prize in the competition between care/desire and Nora/Holly: William's choice to stay at home with Nora even though he pursued his desires elsewhere is offered as a hollow victory for Nora. The verbal fight turns into a food fight and the two collapse into laughter. Their argument leads to a moment of intimacy between them in which Nora tells Holly she needs to let go of William and Holly warns Nora that she should not let her daughter Rebecca live with her.

The scene suggests that the expression of emotion allows people to sort out their differences, however painful and however disparate. However, in *Brothers & Sisters*, this use of emotion comes across in a very sentimentalised way and may leave a viewer wondering how real this proposed solution really is or could be. Perhaps it is cathartic and hopeful and provides viewers with a 'melodramatic fantasy' of family.[4] As Ien Ang suggests: 'Fantasy and fiction then, are the safe spaces of excess in the interstices of ordered social life where one has to keep oneself strategically under control' (1997: 164). In the fantasy world of *Brothers & Sisters* a food fight can magically resolve betrayal and infidelity and restores Nora's place as the central figure in the family drama.

As in *Six Feet Under*, daughters are represented as possessing different agendas and capabilities in the next generation. Sarah Whedon (Rachel Griffiths), Nora's eldest daughter, is both mother (to two children and a step-son) and the President of her late father's company. Unlike her mother, Sarah is seen as able to be both mother and career woman, although this is often troubled by her relationship with her husband, Joe, who has chosen to live at home and look after the children and who, towards the end of the first season, kisses her newly found half-sister, Rebecca. We know that Rebecca is not the victim she pretends to be, and indeed it was Joe that stopped any further relations between them. Through Joe's recollections we see Rebecca telling him that he does not need to stop, even though we later see her tell the brothers and sisters a different story. If Nora and Holly are held in contrast with each other then so too are Sarah and Rebecca, particularly over Joe. Nora tells Sarah that she does not want her to make the same mistakes, that is, stand blindly next to a man who is cheating on her. And yet, as viewers we know that there is more to the story than meets the eye. The storyline suggests that Sarah will end up making her own mistakes in the process of avoiding her mother's mistakes and emphasises the way in which the knowledge from one generation emotionally and intimately parallels the next. Holly's daughter Rebecca is, in essence, destroying a family in the same way that Holly did, but this time Rebecca is acting from a position of pain, having been denied the truth of her parentage, rather than one of passion.

Also similar to the storyline in *Six Feet Under*, Nora's desire is conditional on the family's wellbeing. She only purses her love interests when all other members of the family are happily living their lives. As soon as one of them has a crisis, which happens often, she leaves her romantic pursuits and heads for the kitchen: to make them a sandwich, pour a glass of wine or just listen. Although all her children are fully grown, she is still intimately bound to their happiness and needs. But this relationship is not just a reflection of what popular culture envisions as a 'good mother' – it is also what guarantees her a place in the programme. She is the central character – like the kitchen to a home, she is the person who draws everyone together and unites them.

When Nora confronts Sarah about Joe's affair, Sarah replies that although she realises now that her parents did not have a perfect marriage, she is grateful they stayed together because it made her feel 'whole' and wants to offer the same to her children. Nora tells her that she is a 'good mother'. Here lies the tension between desire and care: Sarah chooses to put her own desires second to her children's wellbeing and this, in part, is what makes her a good mother in Nora's estimation.

The discussion takes place in the kitchen of the winery which will later be the same setting for Holly and Nora's food fight. Again, the kitchen, the domestic centre, is the setting for intimate discussions on mother-hood, caretaking and desire and the location where generations of women reflect on the joys and struggles of homemaking. There is an implicit suggestion here that Sarah has not only become a good mother but will also take her mother's place, literally in the kitchen, as the person who will care for the family alongside her own desires.

Caretaker, mother, homemaker

In her essays on female body experience, Iris Marion Young discusses a series of interlinked essays by feminist scholars on the concept of home. Specifically, she refers to Biddy Martin and Chandra Mohanty's 'Feminist politics: what's home got to do about it?' (1986), which focuses on Minnie Bruce Pratt's experience growing up in the American South as a privileged white woman, and on Teresa de Lauretis's response to Mohanty and Martin, which, as Young points out, further develops the connection between home and identity (2005: 146). What Young finds in these essays and others is a profound distrust of the concept of home within feminist politics and a suggestion that we, as feminists, give up on the desire for home altogether (ibid.: 146), par-ticularly insofar as the home is a privilege bound by class and race. Drawing on bell hooks's discussion of 'homeplace', Young argues that the values of home 'can have a political meaning as a site of dignity and resistance' and should be 'democratised rather than rejected' (ibid.: 146). Although Young agrees that 'the attempt to protect the personal from the political through boundaries of home more likely protects privilege from self-consciousness, and that the personal identities embodied in home inevitably have political implications' (ibid.: 149), she argues for a more fluid notion of home – one that 'does not impose the personal and the political, but instead describes conditions that make the political possible' (ibid.: 149). Following hooks, Young sees a radical potential in the notion of home insofar as it can offer resist-ances and, that if home is a privilege, then it should be extended to everyone, rather than rejected. She imagines the home, not as a nostal-gic longing for comfort and security, but as a real place for individuals to negotiate both personal and collective identities.

Both *Six Feet Under* and *Brothers & Sisters* are very similar, not only in their storylines, characters and actors but also in the way the mother figure becomes central to the emotional fabric of the text. In each series, the matriarch is firmly rooted in the home until the death of her husband. At this point she is freed from her position and yet all her forays into the outside world are seen as inappropriate or failures, implying that her true place is in the home. Most shots are of either Ruth or Nora in the kitchen – the hub of the family home. The kitchen, an archetypical domestic setting, is where intimate discussions on caretaking, motherhood and desire take place. When each woman attempts to find desire with another man she ends up with someone who wants her to take care of him, someone who is more interested in his own desires. Likewise, these moments of sexual freedom are often punished when one of her children calls her to be there for them. In both series daughters emphasise the differences between the genera-tions, the choices that feminism has created and the mistakes that are inherited despite best intentions. The relationship between the mothers and daughters demonstrates the remaining problems and challenges that face women as they struggle to balance home and career: care and desire. At the end of *Six Feet Under* viewers witness Ruth returned to the position in which she began – as caretaker and as responsible for the wellbeing of her family. Because *Brothers & Sisters* is still in produc-tion it is impossible to make the same pronouncement of Nora, although every indication suggests that her role as caretaker, mother and homemaker will continue to frame her sexuality rather than her desires. In both examples, the mother role is pivotal in terms of the emotional storylines in the series. She is the one the other characters turn to, confide in and hide things from. As I have argued, these mother characters are not offered much by way of their own desires which reiterates their position as a device to centre the emotional heart of the programmes.

In an episode from the second series of *Brothers & Sisters* (2.13), for instance, appropriately titled 'Separation Anxiety', Issac (Danny Glover) asks Nora if she will move to his home in DC. In typical fashion, all the children call each other on their mobiles to pass on the latest gossip. They all appear at the house while Nora and Issac are having a romantic, candlelight meal together. He shows her photos of his house and his boat, to entice her to come with him. Later at Rebecca's birthday party, hosted by Nora, the children continue to fret over how they will live without their mother: the children are horrified to discover that Nora has not cooked the food herself, and instead has served store-bought cuisine, which causes Kevin to cry.

Kitty tells Issac that he should not do this to Nora and undermines any confidence he has in Nora's ability to make her own choices. The following dialogue exemplifies the way in which feelings are used in a divisive way:

ISSAC: You have strong feelings about your mother moving away.

KITTY: Issac, this is a woman who needs her family around her. If she goes through with this, I'm afraid you're both going to regret it.

ISSAC: What do you want me to do? Tell a grown woman she doesn't know her feelings?

KITTY: Well feelings don't have anything to do with it – you have clearly swept her off her feet. I just know things about my mother that you don't and if you did I think you would know that you're asking too much.

Here feelings and intimacy are pitted against each other. Kitty dismisses Issac and Nora's feelings for each other because she argues they are temporary; whereas her intimate knowledge and love for her mother is not only permanent but more important than her mother's desires.

Upstairs in the intimacy of her mother's bedroom, Kitty tells her: 'Please don't go, I need you.' Most viewers can guess what follows: Nora tells Issac she cannot move to DC and the relationship is over, along with her passion. The episode ends with Nora eating alone at the dining room table. The meal is contrasted with the romantic (albeit interrupted) dinner she had with Issac. No longer in a low-cut blouse and eating by candlelight, Nora is shown in a cardigan with all the lights on – eating a sad piece of salmon and pretending to be happy. Nora's role is reiterated as mother, caretaker and homemaker and not as lover.

In both series discussed, the mother figure is the caretaker above all else but also the person everyone comes to with their emotional needs and revelations. In so doing, the mother figure provides the series with a character that not only unites the cast but also privileges and fosters intimate and emotional moments. The death of the patriarch is symbolic in that it marks an explicit engagement with the domestic and further suggestion of the feminisation of television.

Notes

1. Special thanks to the Women, Ageing and Media (WAM) Research Group and Julia Hallam for their help in formulating these ideas.

2. Vicki Ball problematises Brunsdon's account of the feminisation of television and argues instead that 'the feminisation of television marks the de-gendering of spaces and discourses associated with the "feminine" in order to appeal to a diverse range of audiences within an increasingly competitive and uncertain context of broadcasting' (2007: 39).
3. See Whelehan 2005.
4. See Ang 1997; Smith 1995: 96–8.

Further discussion/Exercises

1. How does the mother figure foster emotion in another series? Can you think of examples where the mother figure discourages emotional relationships?
2. This chapter considered the way the mother figure becomes a device for emotional and affective moments in series. Can you think of another figure used within television series and consider their function?
3. Do you agree that television is being feminised? In what ways? Think of examples.

Further reading

Arthurs, Jane (2004), *Television and Sexuality*, Buckinghamshire: Open University Press.
Brunsdon, Charlotte (2006), 'The feminist in the kitchen: Martha, Martha and Nigella', in Joanne Hollows and Rachel Moseley (eds), *Feminism in Popular Culture*, Oxford: Berg, pp. 41–56.
Hermes, J. (2006), '"*Ally McBeal*", "*Sex in the City*" and the tragic success of feminism', in J. Hollows and R. Moseley (eds), *Feminism in Popular Culture*, Oxford: Berg, pp. 79–96.
Hollows, Joanne (2006) 'Can I go home yet? Feminism, post-feminism and Domesticity', in Rachel Moseley and Joanne Hollows (eds), *Feminism and Popular Culture*, Oxford: Berg, pp. 97–118.
Honig, Bonnie (1994), 'Difference, dilemmas and the politics of home', *Social Research*, 61(3): 563–97.
McRobbie, Angela (2004), 'Post-feminism and popular culture', *Feminist Media Studies*, 4 (3): 255–64.
Martin, Biddy and Chandra Mohanty (1986) 'Feminist politics: What's home got to do with it?', in Teresa de Lauretis (ed.), *Feminist Studies/Cultural Studies*, Bloomington, IN: Indiana University Press, pp. 191–212.
Modleski, Tania (1982), *Loving with a Vengeance: Mass Produced Fantasies for Women*, Hamden, CT: Archon Books.

Radway, Janice (1984), *Reading the Romance: Women, Patriarchy & Popular Literature*, Chapel Hill, NC: University of North Carolina Press.

Young, Iris (2005), *On Female Body Experience: "Throwing Like a Girl" and Other Essays*, Oxford: Oxford University Press.

10 Researching Emotion in Television: a small-scale case study of emotion in the UK/Irish soap industry

The previous chapters have drawn on particular televisual examples in order to explore how emotion is developed, constructed and valued within television. It has considered how emotion can be fashioned for a reaction from the audience, how particular characters are used to elicit emotional intimacy and how specific textual elements are used to draw in viewers emotionally. The final chapter considers how the industry values the concept of emotion by drawing on interviews with those working within the UK/Irish Television Industry. To begin, however, I shall consider the role of ethnography within television studies and outline the initial set-up of a small-scale case study.

Bird's work in the *Audience in Everyday Life* draws on her research within the field and, in so doing, offers her readers a useful way to consider ethnographic research and cautions against certain kinds of projects. She tells her reader that:

> Rather than worry about relatively insignificant issues like time spent in the field, I believe we should be thinking more carefully about matching suitable methods to the subtle questions we are trying to ask. Our aim should be to achieve an 'ethnographic way of seeing' . . . whose goal Emerson, Fretz and Shaw (1995) define as 'to get close to those studied as a way of understanding what their experiences and activities *mean to them*'. (Bird 2003: 8, italics in original)

What Bird, via others, suggests is that we cannot rely on one methodological approach alone. Instead we must continue to ask questions about our area of research. Similarly, in *Decoding Culture* (1999) Andrew Tudor argues for 'an approach to research which recognizes that all methods for generating descriptive accounts (participant observation, ethnographic interview, questionnaires, historical narrative, statistical analysis, etc.) constitute starting points, individually and collectively, for explanatory analysis' (1999: 176). He understands that each project does not constitute an end in itself, but rather one of many 'starting points' that aim to deepen our understanding of any one issue.

Henry Jenkins points out that there is no privileged position that the researcher should take, rather different vantage points from which he can consider his ideas (1992: 4). This seems a useful approach and one that is in line with the others discussed. No one project is capable of answering the big questions we are asking; it is just one attempt in many to get towards an understanding of the issues at hand. This project is approached within this context. It does not attempt to be conclusive and is unlikely to be so given its small scale. Instead it is designed as a way to open up the issues regarding viewers' emotional engagement with television. It is the first in a series of attempts to consider this question and the possible responses. As Bird argues: 'These kinds of analyses, focused on small-scale exploration of individuals' process of meaning-making, can take us in directions that are quite different from conceptions of the static audience' (2003: 6). Indeed, the value in projects like this one is to validate the notion of an active audience, particularly against allegations of the 'dumbing down' of television programming.

Small-scale case study on audience and emotion

There are numerous ways to approach the concept of emotion in television, as this book has explored: for example, we can consider it theoretically, we can examine its representation in television, and we can consider the formal qualities in a text which encourage emotional engagements. This chapter will extend this discussion in considering how we might explore emotion in the audience through ethnography. Given the scope of this book, this chapter will limit itself to one-to-one semi-structured interviews with industry professionals in the UK/Irish soap industry.

When I initially began the research I intended on interviewing groups of people to record their emotional responses to television programmes. I imagined interviewing people in their homes, so I could also consider the way in which they 'orientate' themselves towards the screen. I was interested in whether they 'set the scene' (by dimming the lights or cuddling up in a blanket) or whether they just watched the programme with other distractions in the background. I also intended asking participants to keep a journal of their television watching habits and emotional responses. I was aware that writing in a journal might provide them with a 'safer' more 'private' space to consider their emotional attachments (as opposed to a structured interview). My initial model of research was loosely based on David

Morley's work in *Family Television* (1986). Morley interviewed eighteen families in their homes in order to consider how television was viewed within the domestic scene. His aim was 'to formulate a position from which we can see the person actively producing meanings from the restricted range of cultural resources which his or her structural position has allowed them access to' (1986: 43). Given some of the similarities between Morley's project and my own, I initially wanted to model my study on his. However, after a few trials, I realised that it was impossible to 'sit in' on the emotional moments people experience when watching television. Part of the experience involves the sense that one is alone or in an intimate surrounding. Having an interviewer at someone's side, recording and observing, breaks this feeling of intimacy.

Following this trial, I decided to focus instead on the industry and its valuation and use of emotion. In particular I examined the soap industry; soaps have traditionally been devalued for their links to the emotional and feminine and although these gendered assumptions have been challenged, many still associate soaps with excess and emotion. John Ellis argues that.

> soap scenarios open up major emotional questions to scrutiny . . . Soaps do so through the combination of empathy that accompanies narrative with a large degree of discussion of any one situation by the whole range of the soap's characters. Such a combination is possible because of the regular and slow-moving nature of the form. (2002: 111)

Indeed, as Sonia Livingstone writes, 'a soap opera lasts indefinitely, making all the more obvious the ways in which viewers must hold the "text" in their memories, integrating across episodes' (1998 [1990]: ix). In the start of her chapter on 'the case of the soap opera', Livingstone also points out that 'Academic revaluation of the soap opera provided a major impetus for re-conceptualising the television audience as active and informed' (ibid.: 51). It therefore seems apt, in a book on television audiences, to focus on soaps in particular.

My experience demonstrates some of the problems one might encounter when setting up an ethnographic study. However, there is always value in attempts to research a particular question, even if you decide to change the focus. I learned from my initial studies that intimacy is often an important factor in a viewer's emotional engagement with television. I also learned that my observation could have an adverse affect on the viewer's emotional experience. As Tudor (1999) has pointed out – the best way to think about ethnographic projects is to consider each attempt as one attempt towards getting a better picture of your research question. Rarely is one study enough from which to draw conclusions and the combination of theoretical, textual and ethnographic approaches best helps to inform us of the directions and questions a research project can and does inspire.

I have conducted focus groups with my students around a particular programme or episode and found that they rarely respond in the same way to the emotion in the text. Perhaps part of the reason for this comes from the information and experiences they bring with them to the viewing process. In his theorisation of the Freudian concept 'working through,' for instance, John Ellis gestures towards the difficulties in separating what the viewers bring to a televisual text from what they take from it (2002: 74–83), and from the responses I have had this seems plausible. For this reason, I have decided to focus instead on the value of emotion placed both in the industry and as perceived by the viewer.

Production, writing, viewing

Robin Nelson argues that:

> Those readers primarily interested in the TV dramas themselves might think the industry background to be less compelling. But, properly to understand why we get a particular kind of TV drama to appear on our screens at any given time is not just a matter of creative people coming up with fresh ideas. (2007: 54)

As Nelson points out, the industry has a lot to do with what we watch and how we watch it and this is particularly true when it comes to emotion. Getting an emotional response is what the industry desires from its viewers, it is what will keep us on a particular channel or get us to buy a DVD box set.

> What we value is the ephemeral transfer of an imagined life from the author's mind to our own, the few minutes of emotion provoked by a song, or the hour and a half we spend in another world conjured up by light coloured light moving across the screen. (Grant and Wood 2004, cited in Nelson 2007: 65)

Indeed, as Kay Mellor (13/6/5) suggests, viewers want to be taken on an emotional 'journey' and often expect that from what they watch (see Chapter 6).

Participants from the UK/Irish television industry

Dr Brigie de Courcy, Executive Producer of *Fair City* (former Senior Story Producer of *EastEnders*)

Kevin McGee, Series Television Writer for *Fair City* and Story Consultant

Anita Turner, Series Producer of *Emmerdale*

Belinda Johns, Development Producer for Rollem Productions

Lisa Holdsworth, Series Writer for *New Tricks*, *Waterloo Road* and *Robin Hood*

Steve Frost, Head of Continuing Series, Drama (former Series Producer of *Coronation Street*), ITV

The interviews reflected an interest and awareness of emotion: its ability to make the viewing experience pleasurable, to draw the viewers in and the way in which it is often constructed or manipulated to elicit a response. Most participants felt emotion came from close attention to the characters, rather than the audience themselves. Kevin McGee, for instance, explains that: 'we're always looking for what the emotion is, but you tend to be talking about the characters rather than the audience'. Nonetheless, emotion remains a primary focus, as Anita Turner suggests: 'Emotion is central. Because I think it defines character, absolutely. You don't have a character if you don't have an emotion, because that's where the truth is.'

The rules of soap

> I have now worked on three distinct soaps – *Emmerdale*, *EastEnders* and *Fair City*, and people die in each one of them . . . but they're told completely differently. (de Courcy)

As de Courcy points out, all soaps, indeed all television programmes, have different ways of telling their stories. They have 'rules' for each programme that are instrumental in the kinds of things writers, directors and producers can do with the show itself. In writing for *Robin Hood*, Holdsworth explains the following:

> I had something in a treatment I did for *Robin Hood* where he walked away from having set two tigers on some faceless non-speaking soldiers, and I wrote that he walked away smiling having escaped from them. But then I got a note saying, 'Robin doesn't smile about killing'. So there are certain unassailable things to certain characters and programmes. *House* probably has a rule that

House is never sentimental; he would never say the words, 'I love you', for instance. But sometimes those rules are grey, so you have the rules and you think, 'How can I break them?' 'How can I get away with it.'

As Holdsworth explains, there are rules in each programme that need to be adhered to, and yet which writers will often try to bend in order to tell the story in a new way. In soaps, there are many rules to take into consideration, particularly when we think of some of the devices used to construct emotion discussed in Chapters 4, 8 and 9. Because soaps attract both faithful and casual viewers, they must repeat certain elements while making sure they are faithful to the history of the programme. De Courcy explains:

> Every episode will have new viewers, who might be just flipping past, and have no idea of the history of the soap and the history of the characters . . . So it's really important to have every episode with huge energy, huge emotional tugs, huge turning points, points of identification for the audience . . . The grammar is that it runs over one day. You don't go overnight, so it is a day in the lives of these people. The rhythm of every week will make sure that you have some complete stories that are resolved then inspires new story . . . there is a constant rolling journey for character and story.

McGee echoes this in saying that 'soaps are about relentless forward motion and discordant emotion'. He goes on to explain that:

> Characters should enter a scene with an attitude to each other and leave with a different attitude to each other, but it's always an emotional attitude and it's always somehow discordant . . . End a scene where both characters have decided that they're in love with each other, no question arises from that story – the scene has resolved that story for the viewer and therefore it's not tugging you forward into the soap, into the future of the drama.

One of the most interesting distinctions made by the participants regarding the difference between dramas and soaps is that soap is often story driven, whereas dramas are character led (Turner). Turner, Series Producer of *Emmerdale*, pointed out that soaps need to work towards distinct annual markers: Christmas, Easter, Summer etc.; therefore the story has to work towards delivering a climactic moment at each one of these points. Often this means the story drives the programme and characters must get on board where it best suits the story. Turner stressed the importance of remaining true to the individual character's emotional journeys but acknowledged that sometimes the importance of delivering the story takes precedence over an individual character's motivation. Her distinction helps us to think about the way in which emotion is focused differently in soaps and dramas. In a drama series, such as those explored in Chapter 8, emotion is tied around the characters and their individual stories. In soaps, the emotion is built into the story.

And yet, as Turner explains, sometimes soaps will adopt this attention to one character in order to construct a long story arc that will deliver emotion along the way until the final climatic moment. For example, she remembers a story conference on *Coronation Street* at which a decision was made to take a particular character and write a story in which he would slowly break down over five years. The central question then becomes 'what are the steps to that point?' Turner explains that one writer would come up with an idea of the story's trajectory for three weeks, and then the story office would take it away and say '"Yeah, OK, that's gonna keep the audience interested", or "OK, we'll play it down a bit because they're gonna start getting too much of a hint, we're going to play the story too quickly".' The construction of emotional involvement in this example has a lot to do with the pace at which the story is told. If details are offered too quickly, then the story is blown and the viewers are no longer interested. This construction of emotion is something that Lisa Holdsworth also alludes to in her discussion of television drama. In analysing the first series of *Heroes*, Holdsworth argues that:

> Every twist and turn needed to come from the plot . . . I think what they did wrong in the second series is that you had grown to love these characters, and therefore wanted to see something that was contradictory to what you knew about them . . . even something upsetting, leading to an exclamation of 'I can't believe he's just done that' is pleasurable for the audience; but you need a run-up to it, to build it up . . . And that's a problem with television at the moment – things are falling at the first hurdle. You just don't have time to invest in the characters.

Attention to characters is seen as central to a viewer's engagement with a programme. Holdworth's suggestion that audiences want to see contradiction in their characters suggests a desire to know more about them. However, McGee suggests that:

> you trust that the audience care about the characters, so that what emotionally affects the characters will emotionally affect the audience, and you try and justify that trust by designing characters that

people will care about, but once you've done that you don't tend to be chasing the audience in any way.

McGee's point that soaps do not need to 'chase the audience' is echoed in Frost's impression of the differences between drama and soap. He argues that there is more room in soaps to explore the characters because most viewers have already made a commitment to watch the programme:

> People watch soaps habitually, it's a habit, and there's almost more time because you've got your audience in a way, you've kind of sold them on the proposition . . . It's very easy to have half an hour of soap where not a lot happens, because viewers want to spend some time with their favourite characters, almost just like meeting your friends, really.

As Frost suggests, the habitual nature of soap viewing means that viewers are often more inclined to 'spend time' with their favourite characters and are less concerned with story.

Everyday people

One of the distinctive features of soaps is the fact that they feature 'ordinary people.' As de Courcy notes: 'the people of soap are very ordinary people . . . and so the emotion and the conflict is driven from the minutiae of living rather than great big outside things'. Soaps are about people's everyday lives and, as such, do not feature extraordinary events. For this reason, they have appealed to a wide range of viewers and to feminist theorists such as Tania Modleski (2008 [1979]), Charlotte Brunsdon (2000a), Christine Geraghty (1990) and Martha Nochimson (1992), who have reclaimed the genre. McGee explains that: 'there's no character that's bigger than a soap . . . which means you can turn characters inside out and destroy their lives and make them unusable, you can kill them and still . . . the show goes on'. The ordinariness of soaps is very different from a dramatic series such as *The Sopranos* where the death of one of the ensemble cast (such as 'Tony' or 'Carmela') would make it difficult for the 'show to go on'.

How does this 'everydayness' affect the emotional engagements viewers have with their favourite soaps? In her work on 'effeminate feelings and pop-culture forms', Warhol reflects on the reasons she enjoys watching soap operas. Given the nature of her peripatetic childhood and early career as an academic, moving from state to state – the only consistent people in her life were the characters on the American soap *As The World Turns* (2003: 103). This experience leads Warhol to question what it *feels* like to 'follow a soap over a period of many years' and how 'those feelings inflect the experience of longtime viewers' (ibid.: 108). She argues that:

> Part of the appeal of following a soap opera over a long period of time is the accumulation of knowledge of those emotive details that add layers of affect to each new episode – when the writers remember to capitalise on that effect. (ibid.: 113)

The knowledge that Warhol refers to is similar to the 'familiarity' discussed in relation to *ER* and *The Sopranos* in Chapter 8. Knowing a character's affective history adds deeper levels of emotional engagement. This is heightened in soap because of the sheer volume of output and long-running histories of the programmes. The ordinariness of the characters also means that their experiences will be more accessible to a broader range of people. Turner discussed a storyline on 'cot death' that generated a significant number of letters. In one letter a woman explained that she and her husband were unable to talk about losing their child until they watched a story about it on a soap opera. Watching the story about other people enabled them to talk about their own experiences.

Identification

One of the issues that concerned me as I began my research was whether the concept of identification, initially used within film studies, influenced in turn by psychoanalytic theories, could be used to describe emotional engagements in television. All the participants, many of whom had learned the concept of identification through BA degrees in film and television studies, dismissed this term as irrelevant and instead preferred to think about the ways viewers related to character's situations or stylistic forms such as close-up shots and other technical devices that aided a relationship between spectator and screen. McGee, for instance, argues that: 'the idea of identification . . . the old-fashioned or layman's idea of identification as being based on some perceived similarity with the character . . . I think that's almost irrelevant. I think the primary reason for identifying with someone is they're on screen'. As McGee suggests, it is the character's very presence on screen that begins the interest a viewer might have, and then this is extended through story, close-up shots, music et al. Belinda Johns points out that:

If you speak to any good director or writer/dramatist, the most effective way to engage the viewer is through close-up shot. For the same reason you may look into someone's eyes if you want to reach them emotionally – a director or writer would establish this through the camera.

These conversations reiterated the importance of thinking beyond the concept of identification in terms of how audiences engage with what they watch. It is not simply that a viewer sees a character and *identifies* with them, rather it is a more complex process in which the emotional situation the character is in elicits a response while, at the same time, technical devices such as a close-up shot or music aids and develops this connection. Frost argues that 'the kind of identification shifts with the situations that people are in' and argues that 'it's about making the emotions recognisable'. His point reiterates Murray Smith's (see Chapter 5) suggestion that viewers's identify with the emotional situations in which characters are, rather than the character him or herself.

New viewing practices and branding

All the participants agreed that changes in technology mean a difference in the way viewers consume television. As Holdsworth pointed out, programmes can no longer hope to get ratings such as *Morecambe and Wise* could command on Christmas Day. Now programmes are lucky if they have a viewing figure reaching 8 million and this has changed both the parameters within drama and the way the industry measures what audiences think about a particular programme. It has also changed the notion of the 'watercooler effect'. Holdsworth and de Courcy both discussed the ways in which people now analyse television on chat forums or on 'digital spy' while the programme is aired. As de Courcy explains:

> One of the things we're up against is people now have Sky Box . . . and that's so much easier than video . . . so it means that the following day the idea of the water-cooler moment, where everybody goes in saying, 'Oh my God, did you see . . . ' that's actually diminished radically because people aren't watching it all at the same time, and they're not all actually buying into it at the same time, but the other thing that is now creeping in, and this is in a much, much younger audience, and you can see it online, is that they're . . . able to process so many threads of information at the same time, they will watch television while on their computer, talking to their mates in DigitalSpy or whatever, and they're talking about the show as

they're watching it and they're typing away like mad, and if you actually hook on to – you can see their responses and this is also how we'll know how people are responding to us . . . they're literally watching it in real-time, and that's the thing that's going to bring us back our water cooler moments, or that's the thing that gives them a shared [feeling] rather than the whole family sitting down to watch *EastEnders* as they used to do at 8 o'clock . . . they now have a virtual family through the internet . . . which is quite interesting for us.

As de Courcy points out, new viewing practices mean new communities of television viewers are emerging. These new practices also mean new ways for the television industry to monitor what viewers enjoy or do not enjoy about particular programmes.

New viewing practices have also led to what Holdsworth sees as a kind of 'branding' of television. She explains that both friends and colleagues often say: '"Oh, you liked *The Wire*, well maybe you should get into *Life on Mars*" or "If you liked *The Sopranos* then you should watch *Mad Men* because it has the same writer".' People are branding shows based either on the style of the programme or on the writer. The issue of branding has been taken up by academics such as Catherine Johnson who argues that HBOs output can be analysed as brands and as part of a consumer-driven television (2007). Frost extends this view of television branding to include the channel itself. He explains:

I think it's increasingly important in creating the appointment to view, in keeping something in an audience's mind, that something has a very strong brand, and not just the individual programme but more the channel, that the channel has a brand. When there are so many channels, so many places to watch, you've got to create a sense of what you're going to get from the channel. In other words, the channel itself can't just be a kind of a platform on which there's a fairly random selection of programmes, it has to have its own logic, its own brand, it has to be identifiable as offering a certain sort of experience.

Frost reiterates the importance of the channel to have its own 'brand' or 'feeling' that viewers come to expect and associate with.

Writing emotion

Following from an interview with Kay Mellor, discussed in Chapter 6, I was interested in talking to the participants about their experiences of writing for television and, more specifically, the ways in which they might 'write emotion' into the text. I asked them how they knew when they had achieved that emotional moment. McGee told me: 'There's a little cruelty when you write something sad, you're not writing with a tear in your eye, you're writing with a big grin on your face.' In describing her experiences as a story producer, de Courcy said: 'You know when you've got the big moment, don't you?' These admissions tell us something about the desire of a writer and producer to elicit emotion from their viewers. Why? Because in so doing they have captured their attention and moved them in a way that might make a viewer remember the experience. Part of the reason why writers and producers seek emotion from their audiences is so that their work is remembered and valued. Emotion is one of the ways this can be achieved. If you think about television moments you remember, it is most likely that you will recall one that moved you in some way. You might remember the storyline, the music or the way something was said. But often it is attached to an emotional moment.

Conclusion: jeopardy and journey

The two words most often used by the participants to discuss the concept of emotion were 'journey' and 'jeopardy'. These two words, used by those working within the industry, refer both to a character's story and to what is at stake in this journey. Holdsworth, for instance, points out that producers will often ask writers to think about 'jeopardy' moments in their storylines. What is at stake? What are the characters risking? These are fundamental questions when considering the emotional dimension of characters and story. As well as valuing the significance of 'journey' to storytelling, Frost also refers to the importance of 'anticipation'. He argues that: 'Anticipation and expectation are really key. If A plus B doesn't lead you to anticipate C, then it's not quite working. You've got to be giving your audience something that makes them anticipate what the next step will be.'

In asking questions about emotion and its value within the television industry, this chapter has reiterated many of the theoretical assertions made in the first half of the book. The value in conducting interviews of this kind is clear in that it allows you to pursue ideas further and to consider more carefully what are often abstract concepts. In other words, it offers some 'grounding' and a new angle on issues already considered. Far more than just 'testing out' ideas, the interviews also led to new concepts and issues to explore. The words 'journey' and 'jeopardy', for instance, offer important ways of thinking about emotion in television. They express the construction (editing, music, close-ups) and the development of emotion in a text that can often lead to an emotional engagement. They also allude to the way emotion orientates us and grabs us – the way it might 'jerk' emotion from us, whether tears, laughter or anger.

Further discussion/Exercises

This chapter has demonstrated some of the issues that arise with ethnography and qualitative research. It has also considered how the UK/Irish television industry values emotion, by drawing on a small number of interviews with industry professionals.

Divide into groups and discuss the different approaches in ethnographic research – what are the problems, limitations and strengths, benefits?

A small-scale case study on emotion and television
As your first piece of research, it is best to keep your project on a small scale. In her excellent work on research practice, Ann Gray reminds us that 'research is always a combination of theorising and a search for the most appropriate and productive methods for our research topic' (2003: 35). Keep this in mind as you attempt your own case study.

Begin by thinking about what aspect of television and emotion you are interested in. What sort of questions does this issue generate? Be careful to use 'open' questions: ones that invite your participant to elaborate on their answer, not ones that encourage a 'yes' or 'no' reply. For instance, instead of asking, 'Do you ever cry when you watch soaps?' (which might be answered with a simple 'yes' or 'no'), ask, 'Describe a moment when you felt emotional about a storyline on a soap opera.'

Once you have decided on your questions, begin with a trial interview, and practice your ideas on friends or family before you attempt to interview your participants.

Use the 'snowballing' technique and ask your friends to ask their friends who would be interested in being interviewed about emotion and television. It is important that you receive written consent from your participants to use the material you gain from the interviews. You must also consult your university's ethics codes and guidelines regarding interviews. Once you have gathered between three and five people willing to be interviewed decide whether you are going to conduct structured interviews, semi-structured interviews, group interviews or focus groups. This decision is partly based on what you want to get out of the research. I conducted one-to-one, semi-structured interviews because I wanted to gather different perspectives from a variety of positions within the television industry and audience.

You might want to examine the emotional response from a

particular programme. For instance, you can ask your participants to watch an episode together and then both observe them and ask them questions about their viewing experience when they are done watching. You can even extend this and conduct one-to-one interviews later. You might also want to ask your participants to write a journal and follow their viewing patterns of one series over the course of its time on air. Or you can lend them a DVD box set of a particular series and ask them to keep notes regarding their emotional involvement as they watch the series. It would be interesting to ask them to write a brief reflection before they start watching about their mood, their feelings of the day – in order to get a sense of what they bring to the text.

Once you have done your interviews, you need to transcribe them. This is often a long process, so be sure to budget your time accordingly. Once you have the transcripts, carefully read through them and highlight common themes among your participants. You should also pay attention to moments of discordance – one participant might have a completely different interpretation of the text to all others.

Drawing from your transcripts and your experience interviewing your participants (self-reflection), write a short essay which summarises your findings.

Further reading

Bird, S. Elizabeth (2004), *The Audience in Everyday Life: Living in a Media World*, New York and London: Routledge.

Brewer, John D. (2000), *Ethnography*, Buckingham: Open University Press.

Denscome, Martyn (1998), *The Good Research Guide: For Small-Scale Social Research Projects*, Buckingham: Open University Press.

Ellis, Carolyn (2004), *The Ethnographic I: A Methodological Novel about Autoethnography*, Walnut Creek, CA: AltaMira Press.

Gray, Ann (2003), *Research Practice for Cultural Studies*, London: Sage.

Jermyn, Deborah (2004), 'In love with Sarah Jessica Parker: celebrating female fandom and friendship in *Sex and the City*', in Kim Akass and Janet Mccabe (eds), *Reading Sex and the City*, London: I. B. Tauris, pp. 201–18.

Schrøder, Kim, Kirsten Drotner, Stephen Kline and Catherine Murray (eds) (2003), *Researching Audiences*, London: Hodder Headline.

Bibliography

Abercrombie, Nicholas and Brian Longhurst (1998), *Audiences*, London: Sage.

Abbott, Paul (2005), 'What do you want to watch tomorrow?', Huw Wheldon Lecture to the Royal Television Society, September.

Abu-Lughod, Lila (2002), 'Egyptian melodrama – technology of the modern subject?', in Faye Ginsburg, Lila Abu-Lughod and Brian Larkin (eds), *Media Worlds: Anthropology on New Terrain*, Berkeley, CA: University of California Press, pp. 115–33.

Adorno, Theodor (1991), *The Culture Industry: Selected Essays on Mass Culture*, ed. J. M. Bernstein, London: Routledge.

Adorno, Theodor and Max Horkheimer (1979), *Dialectic of Enlightenment*, London: Verso.

Ahmed, Sara (2004), *The Cultural Politics of Emotion*, Edinburgh: Edinburgh University Press.

— (2006), *Queer Phenomenology: Orientations, Objects, Others*, Durham, NC: Duke University Press.

— (forthcoming), *The Promise of Happiness*, Durham, NC: Duke University Press.

Alasuutari, Pertti (ed.) (1999), *Rethinking the Media Audience*, London: Sage.

Allen, Robert C. and Annette Hill (eds) (2004), *The Television Studies Reader*, London and New York: Routledge.

Alther, Lisa ([1976] 1999) *Kinflicks*, London: Virago.

Ang, Ien (1985), *Watching Dallas: Soap Opera and the Melodramatic Imagination*, London: Methuen.

— (1991), *Desperately Seeking the Audience*, London: Routledge.

— (1996), *Living Room Wars: Rethinking Media Audiences for a Postmodern World*, London and New York: Routledge.

— (1997), 'Melodramatic identifications: television fiction and women's fantasy', in Charlotte Brunsdon, Julie D'Acci and Lynn Spigel (eds), *Feminist Television Criticism: A Reader*, Oxford: Clarendon Press, pp. 155–66.

Arthurs, Jane (2004), *Television and Sexuality*, Buckinghamshire: Open University Press.

Austin, J. L. (1962), *How to Do Things with Words*, Oxford: Clarendon Press.

Ball, Vicki (2007), 'Female identity and the british female ensemble drama', unpublished PhD dissertation submitted to Queen Margaret University, Edinburgh.

Bandura, Albert and Richard H. Walters (1963), *Social Learning and Personality Development*, New York: Holt, Rinehart and Winston.

Barecca, Regina (2002), *A Sitdown with the Sopranos: Watching Italian American Culture on TV's Most Talked-About Series*, Basingstoke: Palgrave, Palgrave Macmillan.

Barker, Chris (1997), *Global Television: An Introduction*, Malden, MA: Blackwell.

Barker, Martin and Julian Petley (eds) ([1997] 2001), *Ill Effects: The Media/ Violence Debate*, 2nd edn, New York and London: Routledge.

Bauman, Zygmunt (2001), *The Individualized Society*, Cambridge: Polity Press.

Bausinger, Hermann (1984), 'Media, technology and daily life', *Media, Culture and Society*, 6: 343–51.

Bazalgette, Peter (2001), 'RTS Huw Wheldon Memorial Lecture 2001: Big Brother and Beyond', http://www.rts.org.uk/

Beck, Ulrich and Elisabeth Beck-Gernsheim, (2001), *Individualisation: Institutionalized Individualism and Its Social and Political Consequences*, Cambridge: Polity Press.

Berlant, Lawren (1997), *The Queen of America Goes to Washington City: Essays on Sex and Citizenship*, Durham, NC: Duke University Press.

— (ed.) (2000a), *Intimacy*, Chicago, IL: The University of Chicago Press.

Berlant, Lawren (2000b), 'The subject of true feeling: pain, privacy and politics', in S. Ahmed, J. Kilby, C. Lury, M. McNeil and B. Skeggs (eds), *Transformations: Thinking Through Feminism*. London: Routledge, 33–47.

— (2008), *The Female Complaint: The Unfinished Business of Sentimentality in American Culture*, Durham, NC: Duke University Press.

— and Michael Warner (2000), 'Sex in public', in Lauren Berlant (ed.), *Intimacy*, Chicago, IL: University of Chicago Press, pp. 311–51.

Bernstein, J. M. (2001), *Adorno: Disenchantment and Ethics*, Cambridge: Cambridge University Press.

Bianco, Margery Williams (1983), *The Velveteen Rabbit or How Toys Become Real*, New York: Holt, Rinehart and Winston.

Biddle, Jennifer (1997), 'Shame', *Australian Feminist Studies*, 12(26): 227–39.

Bignell, Jonathan (2004), *An Introduction to Television Studies*, London: Routledge.

— and Elke Weissman (2008) 'Cultural difference? Not so different after all', *Critical Studies in Television*, 3(1) Spring: 93–8.

Bird, S. Elizabeth (2003), *The Audience in Everyday Life: Living in a Media World*, New York and London: Routledge.

Biressi, Anita and H. Nunn (2004), *Reality TV: Realism and Revelation*, London: Wallflower Press.

Black, Paula (2006), 'Discipline and pleasure: the uneasy relationship between feminism and the beauty industry', in J. Hollows and R. Moseley (eds), *Feminism in Popular Culture*, Oxford: Berg, pp. 143–59.

Blumler, Jay G. and Elihu Katz (1974), 'Foreword', in J. G. Blumler and Elihu

Katz (eds), *The Uses of Mass Communications: Current Perspectives on Gratifications Research*, Beverly Hills and London: Sage, pp. 13–16.

Blumler, J. G., E. Katz and M. Gurevitch (1974), 'Utilisation of mass communication by the individual', in J. Blumler and E. Katz (eds), *The Uses of Mass Communication: Current Perspectives on Gratifications Research*, New York: Sage, pp. 19–34.

Boddy, William (2005), 'In focus: the place of television studies,' *Cinema Journal*, 45(1): 79–82.

Bonner, Frances (2003), *Ordinary Television: Analyzing Popular TV*, London: Sage.

Bordwell, David (1989), *Making Meaning: Inference and Rhetoric in the Interpretation of Cinema*, Cambridge, MA: Harvard University Press.

Brennan, Teresa (1992), *The Interpretation of the Flesh: Freud and Femininity*, London and New York: Routledge. (Brennan's work is complimented by other projects, such as Wilson 2004, which encourage feminism to embrace neurological accounts of the emotions in that they may offer a more grounded approach to feminist theories of affectivity and embodiment [2004: 83].)

— (2004), *The Transmission of Affect*, Ithaca, NY: University of Cornell Press.

Brewer, John D. (2000), *Ethnography*, Buckingham: Open University Press.

Bright, Susie (2004), *Mommy's Little Girl: On Sex, Motherhood, Porn and Cherry Pie*, New York: Thunder's Mouth.

Bringing Them Home: Report of the National Inquiry into the Separation of Aboriginal and Torres Strait Islander Children from Their Families (1996), Sydney: Human Rights and Equal Opportunities Commission.

Brooker, Will (2002), *Using the Force: Creativity, Community and Star Wars Fans*, New York: Continuum.

Brooker, Will and Deborah Jermyn (eds) (2003), *The Audience Studies Reader*, London: Routledge.

Brooks, Peter (1976), *The Melodramatic Imagination: Balzac, Henry James, Melodrama, and the Mode of Excess*, New Haven, CT: Yale University Press.

Brunsdon, Charlotte (1990), 'Problems with quality', *Screen*, 31(1): 67–90.

— (1998), 'What is the television of television Studies?', in Christine Geraghty and David Lusted (eds), *The Television Studies Book*, London: Arnold, pp. 95–113.

— (2000a), *The Feminist, the Housewife, and the Soap Opera*, Oxford: Oxford University Press.

— (2000b), 'Not having it all: women and film in the 1990s', in Robert Murphy (ed.), *British Cinema of the 90s*, London: British Film Institute, pp. 167–77.

— (2004), 'Lifestyling Britain: the 8–9 slot on British television', in Lynn Spigel and Jan Olsson (eds), *Television after TV: Essays on a Medium in Transition*, Durham: Duke University Press: 75–92. This article originally appeared in (2003) *International Journal of Cultural Studies*, 6(1): 5–23.

— (2006), 'The feminist in the kitchen: Martha, Martha and Nigella', in Joanne Hollows and Rachel Moseley (eds), *Feminism in Popular Culture*, Oxford: Berg, pp. 41–56.

— and David Morley (1978), *Everyday Television: Nationwide*, London: British Film Institute.

Buckingham, D. (1999), 'Researching children's media culture', paper presented at the Conference on Researching Culture, London: University of North London, 12 September.

Buckingham, David (ed.) (2002), *Small Screens: Television for Children*, London and New York: Leicester University Press.

Burton, Graeme (2000), *Talking Television: An Introduction to the Study of Television*, London: Arnold.

Butler, Judith (1990), *Gender Trouble: Feminism and the Subversion of Identity*, New York and London: Routledge.

Byars, Jackie (1991), *All That Hollywood Allows: Rereading Gender in 1950s Melodrama*, London: Routledge.

Caldwell, John Thorton (1995), *Televisuality: Style, Crisis and Authority in American Television*, New Brunswick, NJ: Rutgers University Press.

Cardwell, Sarah (2005), '"Television aesthetics" and close analysis: style, mood and engagement in *Perfect Strangers* (Stephen Poliakoff, 2001)', in John Gibbs and Douglas Pye (eds) *Style and Meaning: Studies in the Detailed Analysis of Film*, Manchester: Manchester University Press, pp. 179–94.

— (2006), 'Television aesthetics', *Critical Studies in Television*, 1(1) Spring: 72–80.

— and Steven Peacock (2006), 'Introduction', special edition *Good Television?*, *Journal of British Cinema and Television*, 3(1): 1–4.

Carroll, Noël (1999), 'Film, emotion, and genre', in Carl Plantinga and Greg M. Smith (eds), *Passionate Views: Film, Cognition, and Emotion*, Baltimore, MD: The Johns Hopkins University Press, pp. 21–47.

Caughie, John (2000), *Television Drama: Realism, Modernism and British Culture*, Oxford: Oxford University Press.

Chodorow, Nancy J. (1999), *The Power of Feelings: Personal Meaning in Psychoanalysis, Gender and Culture*, New Haven, CT: Yale University Press.

Cohen, Stanley ([1972] 2002), *Folk Devils and Moral Panics: The Creation of Mods and Rockers*, 3rd edn, London: Routledge.

Cooke, Lez (2003), *British Television Drama: A History*, London: British Film Institute.

Corcoran, Farrel (2007), 'Television across the world: interrogating the globalisation Paradigm', *New Review of Film and Television Studies*, 5(1): 81–95.

Corner, John (1999), *Critical Ideas in Television Studies*, Oxford: Clarendon Press.

Coward, Rosalind (1984), *Female Desire: Women's Sexuality Today*, London: Paladin.

Creeber, Glen (2004), *Serial Television: Big Drama on the Small Screen*, London: British Film Institute.

Creeber, Glen and Matt Hills (2007), 'Intro, or towards a new television age?', *New Review of Film and Television Studies*, 5(1): 1–4.

Crisell, Andrew (2006), *A Study of Modern Television: Thinking Inside the Box*, Basingstoke: Palgrave Macmillan.

Curran, James and Myung-Jin Park (eds) (2000), *De-Westernizing Media Studies*, London: Routledge.

Curtin, Michael (2003), 'Media capital: towards the study of spatial flows', *International Journal of Cultural Studies*, 6(2): pp. 202–28.

Cvetkovich, Ann (1992), *Mixed Feelings: Feminism, Mass Culture and Victorian Sensationalism*, New Brunswick, NJ: Rutgers University Press.

Cvetkovich, Ann (2003), *An Archive of Feelings: Trauma, Sexuality and Lesbian Public Cultures*, Durham, NC: Duke University Press.

Damasio, Antonio (1994), *Descartes' Error: Emotion, Reason and the Human Brain*, London: Penguin.

— (2003), *Looking for Spinoza: Joy, Sorrow, and the Feeling Brain*, Orlando: Harcourt Books.

Davies, Russell T. (2005), 'Doctor Who confidential: bringing back the doctor', BBC Three, aired on 26 March.

De Certeau, Michel (1984), *The Practice of Everyday Life*, trans. Steven Rendall, Berkeley, CA: University of California Press.

Denscome, Martyn (1998), *The Good Research Guide: For Small-Scale Social Research Projects*, Buckingham: Open University Press.

Devlin-Glass, Frances (2001), 'More than a reader and less than a critic: literary authority and women's book-discussion groups', *Women's Studies International Forum*, 24(5): 571–85.

Doane, Mary Ann (1991), *Femmes Fatales: Feminism, Film Theory, Psychoanalysis*, New York: Routledge.

Eco, Umberto (1986), *Travels in Hyperreality*, London: Picador.

Eldridge, John (1995) (ed.), *Glasgow Media Group Reader; Volume 1: News Content, Language and Visuals*, London and New York: Routledge.

Elliott, Anthony and C. Lemert (2006), *The New Individualism: The Emotional Costs of Globalization*, London: Routledge.

Ellis, Carolyn (2004), *The Ethnographic (I): A Methodological Novel about Ethnography*, Walnut Creek: AltaMira Press.

— (2002), *Seeing Things: Television in the Age of Uncertainty*, London: I. B. Tauris.

Ellis, John (1983), *Visible Fictions*, New York: Routledge.

Elsaeser, Thomas (1992), 'Broadcast television and the social contract,' Lecture given at the University of Hamburg, 23 October, http://home.hum.uva.nl/oz/elsaesser/esssay-television.pdf, accessed 2 March 2007.

Emerson, R. M., R. I. Fretz and L. L. Shaw (1995), *Writing Ethnographic Field Notes*, Chicago, IL: University of Chicago Press.

Eng, David and David Kazanjian (eds) (2003), *On Loss: The Politics of Mourning*, Berkeley, CA: University of California Press.

Evans, Dylan and Pierre Cruse (2004), *Emotion, Evolution and Rationality*, Oxford: Oxford University Press.

Fairclough, Kirsty (2004) 'Women's work? *Wife Swap* and the reality problem', *Feminist Media Studies*, 4(3): 344–6.

Fanon, Franz (1986), *Black Skins, White Masks*, trans, C. L. Markmann, London: Pluto Press.

Fejes, Fred (1981), 'Media imperialism: an assessment', *Media, Culture & Society*, 3: 281–9.

Fiske, John ([1982] 1990), *Introduction to Communication Studies*, 2nd edn, London and New York: Routledge.

— (1987), *Television Culture*, London: Routledge.

— (1989a), *Understanding Popular Culture*, London: Unwin Hyman.

— (1989b), *Reading the Popular*, London: Unwin Hyman.

— (1992), 'The cultural economy of fandom', in Lisa A. Lewis (ed.), *The Adoring Audience: Fan Culture and Popular Media*, London and New York: Routledge, pp. 30–49.

Foucault, Michel (1978), *The History of Sexuality: An Introduction*, trans Robert Hurley, New York: Pantheon.

Gabbard, Glen O. (2002), *The Psychology of The Sopranos: Love, Death, Desire and Betrayal in America's Favorite Gangster Family*, New York: Basic Books.

Gamson, Joshua (1994), *Claims to Fame: Celebrity in Contemporary America*, Berkeley and Los Angeles, CA: University of California Press.

Gauntlett, David (2002), *Media, Gender and Identity: An Introduction*, London: Routledge.

— and Annette Hill (1999), *TV Living: Television, Culture and Everyday Life*, London and New York: Routledge/British Film Institute.

Geraghty, Christine (1990), *Women and Soap Opera: A Study of Prime Time Soaps*, London: Polity Press.

— (2003), 'Aesthetics and quality in popular television drama', *International Journal of Cultural Studies*, 6(1): 25–45.

— and David Lusted (eds) (1997), *The Television Studies Book*, London: Arnold.

Gerbner, G. (1956), 'Towards a general model of communication', *Audio Visual Communication Review*, 4(3): 171–99.

Gibbs, Anna (2001) 'Contagious feelings: Pauline Hanson and the epidemiology of affect', *Australian Humanities Review*, http://www.lib.latrobe.edu.au/AHR/archive/Issue-December-2001/gibbs.html, accessed 3 May 2007.

Giddens, Anthony (1990), *The Consequences of Modernity*, Cambridge: Polity Press.

— (1991), *Modernity and Self-Identity*, Cambridge: Polity Press.

Ginsburg, Faye D., Lila Abu-Lughod and Brian Larkin (eds) (2002), 'Introduction', *Media Worlds: Anthropology on New Terrain*, Berkeley and London: University of California Press, pp. 1–36.

Goldblatt, David (2002), 'Running reruns, vacillating channels: toward an expanded reception theory of television', in Ruth Lorand (ed.), *Television: Aesthetic Reflections*, New York: Peter Lang, pp. 71–88.

Goldie, Peter (2000), *The Emotions: A Philosophical Exploration*, Oxford: Oxford University Press.

Gorton, Kristyn (2004), '(Un)fashionable feminists: the media and *Ally McBeal*', in Stacy Gillis, Gillian Howie and Rebecca Munford (eds), *Third Wave Feminism: A Critical Exploration*, Basingstoke: Palgrave, now Palgrave Macmillan, 154–63.

— (2006), 'A sentimental journey: television, meaning and emotion', *The Journal of British Cinema and Television*, 3(1): 72–81.

— (2007) 'Theorising Emotion and Affect: Feminist Engagements,' *Feminist Theory*, Vol. 8(3): 333–48.

— (2008a) *Theorising Desire: From Freud to Feminism to Film*, London: Palgrave.

— (2008b) '"There's no place like home": emotional exposure, excess and empathy on TV', *Critical Studies in Television*, Vol. 3(1): 3–15.

— (2009a) 'Domestic desire: older women's sexuality in *Six Feet Under* & *Brothers & Sisters*', in Stacy Gillis and Joanne Hollows (eds) *Feminism, Domesticity and Popular Culture*, London and New York: Routledge, pp. 93–106.

— (2009b), 'Why I love Carmela Soprano: ambivalence, the domestic and televisual therapy', *Feminism and Psychology*, 19(1): 128–31.

Grant, P. and C. Wood (2004), *Blockbusters and Trade Wards: Popular Culture in a Globalized World*, Vancouver/Toronto: Douglas & McIntyre.

Gray, Ann (2003), *Research Practice for Cultural Studies*, London: Sage.

Greene, Richard and Peter Vernezze (2004), *The Sopranos and Philosophy: I Kill Therefore I am*, Chicago and LaSalle, IL: Open Court.

Grodal, Torben (1997), *Moving Pictures: A New Theory of Film Genres, Feelings and Cognition*, Oxford: Oxford University Press.

Grossberg, Lawrence (1987), 'The indifference of television', *Screen*, 28(2): 28–45.

— (1992a) 'Is there a fan in the house?: the affective sensibility of fandom', in Lisa A. Lewis (ed.), *Adoring Audience: Fan Culture and Popular Media*, London and New York: Routledge, pp. 50–68.

— (1992b), 'Mapping popular culture', *We Gotta Get Outta This Place: Popular Conservatism and Postmodern Culture*, New York: Routledge, pp. 69–87. (The essays in this collection, some of which were first published in an award-winning issue of *Critical Inquiry*, seek to address the 'contradictory desires' that 'mark the intimacy of daily life' [2000: 5].)

— (1997), *Dancing in Spite of Myself: Essays on Popular Culture*, Durham, NC: Duke University Press (this book is a collection of his essays, one of which is the 1987 essay on the indifference of television).

Gunew, Sneja (2004), *Haunted Nations: The Colonial Dimensions of Multiculturalisms*, London: Routledge.

Gwenllian-Jones, Sara (2003), 'Web wars: resistance, online fandom and studio censorship', in Mark Jancovich and James Lyons (eds), *Quality Popular Television*, London: British Film Institute, pp. 163–80.

— and Roberta Pearson (eds) (2004), *Cult Television*, Minneapolis, MN: University of Minnesota Press.

Hall, Stuart (1974), 'Encoding and decoding in the television discourse', Centre for Contemporary Cultural Studies, Stencilled Occasional Paper No. 7, Birmingham: University of Birmingham.

— (1986), 'Introduction', in David Morley, *Family Television: Cultural Power and Domestic Leisure*, London: Commedia, pp. 7–10.

— ([1980] 2001), 'Encoding/decoding', in Meenakshi Gigi Durham and Douglas M. Kellner (eds), *Media and Cultural Studies: Key Works*, Oxford: Blackwell, pp. 166–76.

Halloran, James (1970), *The Effects of Television*, London: Panther.

Held, David (1980), *Introduction to Critical Theory: Horkheimer to Habermas*, Cambridge: Polity Press.

Hermes, Joke (2005), *Re-reading Popular Culture*, Oxford: Blackwell.

— (2006), '"*Ally McBeal*", "*Sex in the City*" and the tragic success of feminism', in J. Hollows and R. Moseley (eds), *Feminism in Popular Culture*, Oxford: Berg, pp. 79–96.

Heywood, Leslie and Jennifer Drake (1997), 'Introduction', in L. Heywood and J. Drake (eds), *Third Wave Agenda: Being Feminist, Doing Feminism*, Minneapolis, MN: University of Minnesota Press, pp. 1–20.

Hill, Annette (2007), *Restyling Factual TV: Audiences and News, Documentary and Reality Genres*, London: Routledge.

— and Ian Calcutt (2001), 'Vampire hunters: the scheduling and reception of *Buffy the Vampire Slayer* and *Angel* in the UK', *Intensities*, Issue 1.

Hills, Matt (2002), *Fan Cultures*, London and New York: Routledge.

— (2007), 'From the box in the corner to the box set on the shelf: "TV III" and the cultural/textual valorisations of DVD', *New Review of Film and Television Studies*, 5(1): 41–60.

Hilmes, Michelle (2003), *The Television History Book*, London: British Film Institute.

Hobson, Dorothy (1982), *Crossroads: The Drama of a Soap Opera*, London: Methuen.

Hochschild, Arlie R. ([1983] 2003), *The Managed Heart: Commercialization of Human Feeling*, Berkeley, CA: University of California Press.

Hollows, Joanne (2006) 'Can I go home yet? Feminism, post-feminism and domesticity', in (eds), Rachel Moseley and Joanne Hollows, *Feminism and Popular Culture*, Oxford: Berg, pp. 97–118.

Holmes, Susan and Deborah Jermyn (eds)(2004), *Understanding Reality Television*, London: Routledge.

Honig, Bonnie (1994), 'Difference, dilemmas and the politics of home', *Social Research*, 61(3): 563–97.

hooks, bell (1989), *Talking Back: Thinking Feminist, Thinking Black*, London: Sheba Feminist Publishers.

Ill Effects: The Media/Violence Debate, ed. Martin Barker and Julian Petley, London and New York: Routledge, 2001 [1997].

Jacobs, Jason (2000), *The Intimate Screen: Early British Television Drama*, Oxford: Oxford University Press.

— (2006), 'Television aesthetics: an infantile disorder', *Journal of British Cinema and Television*, 3(1): 18–33.

Jagger, Alison M. (1989), 'Love and knowledge: emotion in feminist epistemology', in A. Jagger and S. Bordo (eds), *Gender/Body/Knowledge: Feminist Reconstructions of Being and Knowing*, New Brunswick, NJ: Rutgers University Press, pp. 000–000.

— (1992 [1989]), 'Love and knowledge: emotion in feminist epistemology', in A. Garry and M. Pearsall (eds), *Women, Knowledge and Reality: Explorations in Feminist Philosophy*, London and New York: Routledge, pp. 129–56.

Jancovich, Mark and James Lyons (eds) (2003) *Quality Popular Television*, London: British Film Institute.

Jenkins, Henry (1992), *Textual Poachers: Television Fans & Participatory Culture*, New York and London: Routledge.

— (2001), '*Intensities* interviews with Henry Jenkins and Matt Hills at the Console-ing Passions Conference, University of Bristol, July 7', http://intensities.org, Issue 2.

— (2006), *Fans, Bloggers and Gamers: Exploring Participatory Culture*, New York: New York University Press.

— (2006), *Convergence Culture: Where Old and New Media Collide*, New York and London: New York University Press.

— (2007), *The Wow Climax: Tracing the Emotional Impact of Popular Culture*, New York: New York University Press.

Jermyn, Deborah (2004), 'In love with Sarah Jessica Parker: celebrating female fandom and friendship in *Sex and the City*', in Kim Akass and Janet McCabe (eds), *Reading Sex and the City*, London: I. B. Tauris, pp. 201–18.

Jerslev, Anne (2006), 'Sacred viewing: emotional responses to *The Lord of the Rings*', in Ernest Mathjis (ed.), *The Lord of the Rings: Popular Culture in Global Context*, London and New York: Wallflower Press, pp. 206–24.

Johnson, Catherine (2007), 'Tele-branding in TV III: the network as brand and the programme as brand', *New Review of Film and Television Studies*, 5(1): 5–24.

Johnson, Derek (2007), 'Inviting audiences in: the spatial reorganisation of production and consumption in TV III', *New Review of Film and Television Studies*, 5(1): 61–80.

Jong, Erica ([1973] 1998), *Fear of Flying*, London: Vintage.

Katz, Elihu (1957), 'The Two-Step Flow of Communication: An Up-to-date Report on a Hypothesis,' *Public Opinion Quarterly* Vol. 21(1), pp. 61–78.

Katz, Elihu and Paul F. Lazarsfeld (1964), *Personal Influence: The Part Played by People in the Flow of Mass Communications*, New York: The Free Press.

Katz, Jack (1999), *How Emotions Work*, Chicago, IL: University of Chicago Press.

Kellner, Douglas (1995), *Media Cultures*, London: Routledge.

Kirby, V. (1997), *Telling Flesh: The Substance of the Corporeal*, New York: Routledge.

Kitzinger, Jenny (1999), 'A sociology of media power: key issues in audience reception research', in Greg Philo (ed.), *Message Received*, Harlow: Longman, pp. 2–20.

Knight, Deborah (1999), 'Why we enjoy condemning sentimentality: a meta-aesthetic perspective', *Journal of Aesthetics and Art Criticism*, 57(4): 411–40.

Kompare, Derek (2006), 'Publishing flow: DVD box sets and the reconception of television', *Television & New Media*, 7(4): 335–60.

Lasswell, H. D. (1948), 'The structure and function of communication in society', in L. Bryson (ed.), *The Communication of Ideas*, New York: Institute for Religious and Social Studies.

Lavery, David (ed.) (2002), *This Thing of Ours: Investigating The Sopranos*, London: Wallflower.

— (2006), *Reading The Sopranos: Hit TV from HBO*, London and New York: I. B. Tauris.

Lay, Samantha (2002), *British Social Realism: From Documentary to Brit Grit*, London: Wallflower Press.

Lemish, Dafna (2007), *Children and Television: A Global Perspective*, Oxford: Wiley-Blackwell.

Leverette, Marc, Brian L. Ott and Cara Louise Buckley (eds) (2008), *It's Not TV: Watching HBO in the Post-Television Era*, New York and London: Routledge.

Lewis, Lisa A. (ed.) (1992), *The Adoring Audience: Fan Culture and Popular Media*, London and New York: Routledge.

Liebes, Tamar and E. Katz (1990), *The Export of Meaning: Cross-Cultural Readings of 'Dallas'*, New York: Oxford University Press.

Lila, Abu-Lughod (1986), *Veiled Sentiments: Honour and Poetry in a Bedouin Society*, Berkeley, CA: University of California Press.

Lindner, Christoph (2003) (ed.), *The James Bond Phenomenon: A Critical Reader*, Manchester: Manchester University Press.

Livingstone, Sonia ([1990] 1998), *Making Sense of Television: The Psychology of Audience Interpretation*, 2nd edn, London: Routledge.

— and Peter Lunt (1994), *Talk on Television: Audience Participation and Public Debate*, London: Routledge.

Lorde, Audre (1984), *Sister Outsider: Essays and Speeches*, Trumansburg, NY: The Crossing Press.

Lotz, Amanda D. (2001), 'Postfeminist television criticism: rehabilitating critical terms and identifying postfeminist attributes', *Feminist Media Studies*, 1(1): 105–21.

— and Sharon Marie Ross (2004), 'Bridging media-specific approaches: the value of feminist television's criticism's synthetic approach', *Feminist Media Studies*, 4(2): 185–202.

Lull, James (ed.) (1988), *World Families Watch Television*, London: Sage.

— (2007), 'Television and communicational space: the clash of global hegemonies', *New Review of Film and Television Studies*, 5(1): 97–110.

Lury, Karen (2005), *Interpreting Television*, London: Hodder Headline.

Lutz, Catherine (1988), *Unnatural Emotions: Everyday Sentiments on a Micronesian Atoll and Their Challenge to Western Theory*, Chicago, IL: University of Chicago Press.

McCabe, Janet and Kim Akass (2006), 'What has Carmela ever done for feminism?: Carmela Soprano and the post-feminist dilemma', in David Lavery (ed.), *Reading the Sopranos: Hit TV from HBO*, London and New York: I. B. Tauris, pp. 39–55.

MacCarthy, Anna (2001), *Ambient Television: Visual Culture and Public Space*, Durham, NC: Duke University Press.

McHugh, Kathleen and Vivian Sobchack (2004), 'Introduction', 'Beyond the gaze: recent approaches to film feminisms', *Signs*, 30(1): 1205–8.

McKee, A (2001), 'Which is the best *Dr Who* story?', *Intensities: The Journal of Cult media*, accessed online 18 October 2004 at http://www.cult-media.com/issue1/Amckee.htm.

McQuail, D., J. G. Blumler and J. R. Brown (1972), 'The television audience: a revised perspective', in D. McQuail (ed.), *Sociology of Mass Communications*, Harmondsworth: Penguin.

McRobbie, Angela (2004), 'Post-feminism and popular culture', *Feminist Media Studies*, 4(3): 255–64.

Mankekar, Purnima (1999), *Screening Culture, Viewing Politics: An Ethnography of Television, Womenhood and Nation in Postcolonial India*, Durham, NC: Duke University Press.

Martin, Biddy and Chandra Mohanty (1986), 'Feminist politics: what's home got to do with it?', in Teresa de Lauretis, (ed.) *Feminist Studies/Cultural Studies*, Bloomington, IN: Indiana University Press, pp. 191–212.

Massumi, Brian (2002), *Parables for the Virtual: Movement, Affect, Sensation*, Durham, NC: Duke University Press.

Matravers, Derek (1998), *Art and Emotion*, Oxford: Oxford University Press.

Mellor, Kay (1996), *A Passionate Woman: A Play by Kay Mellor*, London: Samuel French.

Mercer, John and Martin Shingler (2004), *Melodrama: Genre, Style, Sensibility*, London: Wallflower.

Metz, Christian (1975), 'The imaginary signifier', *Screen*, 16(2): 14–76, trans. Ben Brewster.

Miller, Jeffrey (2000), *Something Completely Different: British Television and American Culture*, Minneapolis, MN: University of Minnesota Press.

Miller, Toby (2002), *Television Studies*, London: British Film Institute.

— (2007), *Cultural Citizenship: Cosmopolitanism, Consumerism and Television in a Neoliberal Age*, Philadelphia, PA: Temple University Press.

Modleski, Tania (1982), *Loving with a Vengeance: Mass Produced Fantasies for Women*, Hamden, CT: Archon Books.

— ([1979] 2008), 'The search for tomorrow in today's soap operas: notes on a feminine narrative form', in Charlotte Brunsdon and Lynn Spigel (eds),

Feminist Television Criticism, 2nd edn, Maidenhead: Open University Press, pp. 29–40

Moore, Suzanne (1989), 'Here's looking at you, Kid!', in Lorraine Gamman and Margaret Marshment (eds) *The Female Gaze: Women as Viewers of Popular Culture*, Seattle: The Real Comet Press, pp. 44–59.

Moores, Shaun (1993), *Interpreting Audiences: The Ethnography of Media Consumption*, London: Sage.

Morley, David (1980), *The Nationwide Audience*, London: British Film Institute.

— (1986), *Family Television: Cultural Power and Domestic Leisure*, New York and London: Comedia.

— (1992), *Television, Audiences and Cultural Studies*, London and New York: Routledge.

— (2000), *Home Territories: Media, Mobility and Identity*, London and New York: Routledge.

— (2006), personal conversation with the author.

Moseley, Rachel (2000), 'Makeover takeover on British television', *Screen*, 41(3): 299–314.

Mulvey, Laura (1975), 'Visual Pleasure and Narrative Cinema', *Screen*, 16(3): 6–18.

Naficy, Hamid (1993), *The Making of Exile Cultures: Iranian Television in Los Angeles*, Minneapolis, MN: University of Minnesota Press.

Nelson, Robin (n. d.), *State of Play: Contemporary 'High-End' TV Drama*, Manchester: Manchester University Press.

— (1997), *TV Drama in Transition: Forms, Values and Cultural Change*, Basingstoke: Macmillan, now Palgrave Macmillan.

Newcomb, Horace (2000) (ed.), *Television: The Critical View*, Oxford: Oxford University Press.

— (2005), 'Studying television: same questions, different contexts', *Cinema Journal*, 45(1): 107–11.

Ngai, Sianne (2005), *Ugly Feelings*, Cambridge, MA: Harvard University Press.

Nicholson, Linda (1999), *The Play of Reason: From the Modern to the Postmodern*, Buckingham: Open University Press.

Nightingale, Virginia (1996), *Studying Audiences: The Shock of the Real*, London: Routledge.

— (2007), 'Lost in space: television's missing publics', conference paper delivered at the SCMS conference, Chicago.

Noble, Grant (1975), *Children in Front of the Small Screen*, London: Sage.

Nochimson, Martha (1992), *No End to Her: Soap Opera and the Female Subject*, Berkeley and Los Angeles, CA: University of California Press.

Nussbaum, Martha C. (2001), *Upheavals of Thought: The Intelligence of Emotions*, Cambridge: Cambridge University Press.

Parks, Lisa (2005), *Cultures in Orbit: Satellites and the Televisual*, Durham, NC: Duke University Press.

Pearce, Lynn (2006), 'Book review: *Impersonal Passion: Language as Affect*', *Feminist Theory*, 7(3): 364–5.

Peterson, Alan (2004), *Engendering Emotions*, Basingstoke: Palgrave, now Palgrave Macmillan.

Philo, Greg (1990), *Seeing and Believing: The Influence of Television*, London and New York: Routledge.

— (1995) (ed.), *Glasgow Media Group Reader; Volume 2: Industry, Economy, War and Politics*, London and New York: Routledge.

— (1999a), 'Conclusions on media audiences and message reception', in Greg Philo (ed.), *Message Received*, Harlow: Longman, pp. 282–8.

— (1999b) (ed.), *Message Received: Glasgow Media Group Research 1993–1998*, Harlow: Longman.

— and David Miller (eds) (2001), *Market Killing: What the Free Market Does and What Social Scientists Can Do about It*, Harlow: Pearson Education.

Piper, Helen (2004), 'Reality TV, *Wife Swap* and the drama of banality', *Screen*, 45(4): 273–86.

Plantinga, Carl (1997), 'Notes on spectator emotion and ideological film criticism', in Richard Allen and Murray Smith (eds), *Film Theory and Philosophy*, Oxford: Clarendon Press, pp. 372–93.

— (1999), 'The scene of empathy and the human face on film,' in Carl Plantinga and Greg M. Smith (eds), *Passionate Views: Film, Cognition and Emotion*, Baltimore and London: The Johns Hopkins University Press, pp. 239–56.

— and Greg M. Smith (1999b), *Passionate Views: Film, Cognition and Emotion*, Baltimore and London: The Johns Hopkins University Press.

Pratt, Mary Louise (2008 [1992]), *Imperial Eyes: Travel Writing and Transculturation*, 2nd edn, London and New York: Routledge.

Probyn, Elspeth (2005), *Blush: Faces of Shame*, Minneapolis, MN: University of Minnesota Press.

Radway, Janice (1984), *Reading the Romance: Women, Patriarchy and Popular Literature*, Chapel Hill, NC: University of North Carolina Press.

Riley, Denise (2005), *Impersonal Passion: Language as Affect*, Durham, NC: Duke University Press.

Rixon, Paul (2006), *American Television on British Screens: A Story of Cultural Interaction*, Basingstoke: Palgrave Macmillan.

Robinson, Jenefer (2005), *Deeper Than Reason: Emotion and Its Role in Literature, Music, and Art*, Oxford: Oxford University Press.

Roehrkasse, Alex (2007), '*Battlestar Galactica* Star Discusses Art Mimicking Life', in *The Brown Daily Herald*: 1 (www.browndailyherald.com/media/storage/paper 472).

Rojek, Chris (2001), *Celebrity*, London: Reaktion Books.

Ross, Karen and Virginia Nightingale (2003), *Media and Audiences: New Perspectives*, Maidenhead: Open University Press.

Ruddock, Andy (2001), *Understanding Audiences: Theory and Method*, London: Sage.

Schiller, Herbert I. (1969), *Mass Communications and American Empire*, New York: A. M. Kelley.

Schrøder, Kim, Kirsten Drotner, Stephen Kline and Catherine Murray (2003) (eds), *Researching Audiences*, London: Hodder Headline.

Sedgwick, Eve Kosofsky (2003), *Touching Feeling: Affect, Pedagogy, Performativity*, Durham, NC: Duke University Press.

Seiter, Ellen (2000), 'Making distinctions in TV audience research: case study of a troubling interview', in Horace Newcomb (ed.), *Television: The Critical View*, 6th edn, New York and Oxford: Oxford University Press, pp. 495–518.

Shannon, C. E. and W. Weaver (1963), *The Mathematical Theory of Communication*, Urbana, IL: University of Illinois Press.

Shattuc, Jane (1994), 'Having a good cry over *The Colour Purple*: the problem of affect and imperialism in feminist theory,' in J. Bratton, C. Gledhill and J. Cook (eds), *Melodrama: Stage Picture Screen*, London: British Film Institute, pp. 147–56.

Silverstone, Roger (1994), *Television and Everyday Life*, London and New York: Routledge.

Sinclair, J., E. Jacka and S. Cunningham (1996), *Peripheral Vision: New Patterns in Global Television*, Oxford: Oxford University Press.

Skeggs, Beverley (2004), *Class, Self, Culture*, Routledge, London.

Smith, Greg M. (1999), 'Local emotions, global moods and film structure', in Carl Plantinga and Greg M. Smith, *Passionate Views: Film, Cognition and Emotion*, Baltimore and London: The Johns Hopkins University Press, pp. 103–26.

— (2003), *Film Structure and the Emotional System*, Cambridge: Cambridge University Press.

— (2006), 'A case of cold feet: serial narration and the character arc,' *Journal of British Cinema and Television*, 3(1): 82–94.

— (2007), *Beautiful TV: The Art and Argument of Ally McBeal*, Austin, TX: University of Texas Press.

Smith, Jeff (1999), 'Movie music as moving music: emotion, cognition and the film score,' in Carl Plantinga and Greg M. Smith (eds), *Passionate Views: Film, Cognition and Emotion*, Baltimore and London: The Johns Hopkins University Press, pp. 146–67.

Smith, Murray (1995), *Engaging Characters: Fiction, Emotion and the Cinema*, Oxford: Oxford University Press.

Sobchack, Vivian (2004), *Carnal Thoughts: Embodiment and Moving Image Culture*, Berkeley, CA: University of California Press.

Solomon, Robert C. (ed.) ([1984] 2003), *What Is an Emotion? Classic and Contemporary Readings*, 2nd end, Oxford: Oxford University Press.

— (1993), *The Passions: Emotions and the Meaning of Life*, Indianapolis, IN: Hackett Publishing Company.

— (2004), *In Defense of Sentimentality*, Oxford: Oxford University Press.

Spelman, Elizazbeth V. (1989), 'Anger and insubordination', in A. Garry and

M. Pearsall (eds), *Women, Knowledge, and Reality: Explorations in Feminist Philosophy*, Boston: Unwin Hyman, pp. 263–73.

— (1997), *Fruits of Sorrow: Framing Our Attention to Suffering*, Boston, MA: Beacon Press.

Spigel, Lynn (1992), 'Introduction', *Television: Technology and Cultural Form*, New York and London: ix–xxxvii.

Tan, Ed S. (1996), *Emotion and the Structure of Narrative Film: Film as an Emotion Machine*, Mahwah, NJ: Lawrence Erlbaum Associates, Publishers.

Terada, Rei (2001), *Feeling in Theory: Emotion after the "Death of the Subject"*, Cambridge, MA: Harvard University Press.

Thorburn, David (2000), 'Television melodrama', in Horace Newcomb (ed.), *Television: The Critical View*, 6th edn, Oxford: Oxford University Press, pp. 595–608.

Thornham, Sue (2007), *Women, Feminism and Media*, Edinburgh: Edinburgh University Press.

Tomkins, Silvan Solomon (1962–92), *Affect, Imagery, Consciousness*, with the editorial assistance of Bertram P. Karon, 4 vols, New York: Springer.

— (1995), *Shame and Its Sisters: A Silvan Tomkins Reader*, ed. Eve K. Sedgwick and Adam Frank, Durham, NC: Duke University Press.

Tracey, Michael (1985), 'The poisoned chalice? International television and the idea of dominance', *Daedalus*, 114(4): 17–56.

Tudor, Andrew (1999), *Decoding Culture: Theory and Method in Cultural Studies*, London: Sage.

Warhol, Robyn (2003), *Having a Good Cry: Effeminate Feelings and Pop-Culture Forms*, Columbus, OH: The Ohio State University Press.

Webb, P. (2003), *Wife Swap*, London: Contender Books.

Whelehan, Imelda (2005), *The Feminist Bestseller: From Sex and the Single Girl to Sex and the City*, Basingstoke: Palgrave Macmillan.

Whilde, M. R. (2007), Review of *An Archive of Feelings: Trauma, Sexuality and Lesbian Public Cultures* (Cvetkovich 2003), in *Psychoanalysis, Culture and Society*, 12: 97–9.

White, Rosie (2007), *Violent Femmes: Women as Spies in Popular Culture*, London and New York: Routledge.

Williams, Linda (1991), 'Film bodies: gender, genre and excess,' *Film Quarterly*, 44(4): 2–13.

Williams, Raymond (1961), *The Long Revolution*, London: Chatto & Windus.

— (1989), *Raymond Williams on Television: Selected Writings*, ed. Alan O'Connor, London and New York: Routledge.

— ([1974] 1992), *Television: Technology and Cultural Form*, Hanover: Wesleyan University Press.

— (1977), *Marxism and Literature*, Oxford: Oxford University Press.

Wilson, Elizabeth A. (2004), *Psychosomatic: Feminism and the Neurological Body*, Durham, NC: Duke University Press.

Wood, Helen and Beverley Skeggs (2004), 'Notes on ethical scenarios of self on british reality TV', *Feminist Media Studies*, 4(2): 205–7.

Wood, Helen and Lisa Taylor (2008), 'Feeling sentimental about television audiences,' *Cinema Journal*, 47(3): 144–51.

Woodward, Kathryn (1996), 'Global cooling and academic warming: long-term shifts in emotional weather', *American Literary History* 8(4): 759–79.

Yacowar, Maurice (2003), *The Sopranos on the Couch: Analyzing Television's Greatest Series*, New York: Continuum.

Young, Iris (2005), *On Female Body Experience: "Throwing Like a Girl" and Other Essays*, Oxford: Oxford University Press.

Interviews

13/6/5 – interview with British television writer/producer, Kay Mellor

13/2/8 – interview with a group of post-graduate students at the University of York on the concept of emotion in television (Participants included: Noelani Peace, Martin Zeller, Claire Swarbrick, Junna Wang and Hsaio-Chen Chang)

9/3/8 – interview with Brigie de Courcy and Kevin McGee, *Fair City*, Dublin

23/5/8 – interview with Anita Turner, *Emmerdale*

26/5/8 – interview with Belinda Johns, Rollem Productions

3/6/8 – interview with Lisa Holdsworth, Leeds

8/9/8 – interview with Steve Frost, ITV Drama

Television and Film References

24 (Fox 2001–)

Alien Nation (Fox 1989–90)

Analyze This (Warner Bros 1999)

American Idol (Fremantle Media 2002–)

The Avengers (ITV 1961–9)

Band of Gold (Granada 1996)

Batman (20th Century Fox 1966–8)

Battlestar Galactica (Glen A. Larson 1978–9) and *Battlestar Galactica Reimagined* (BSkyB 2004–)

Between the Sheets (ITV Kay Mellor, 2003)

Big Brother (Endemol 1999–)

The Biggest Loser (NBC 2004–)

Blake's 7 (BBC, Terry Nation, 1978–81)

Boys Don't Cry (Kimberly Pierse 1999)

Boys from the Blackstuff (BBC 1982)

Brothers & Sisters (ABC 2006–)

Cathy Come Home (BBC, Ken Loach, 1966)

Children's Ward (ITV 1998–2000)

Clocking Off (Paul Abbott, BBC 2000–3)

Cold Feet (Granada, Mike Bullen, 1997–2003)

Dallas (Lorimar 1978–91)
Doctor Who (BBC 1963–)
Dr Phil (Harpo Productions 2002–)
The Elephant Man (Lynch 1980)
ER (Michael Crichton, 1994–)
Extreme Makeover (ABC 2002–7)
Family Guy (Seth MacFarlane 1999–)
Fanny and Elvis (Kay Mellor, The Film Consortium, 1999)
Fans and Freaks: The Culture of Comics and Conventions (Lackey 2002)
Fat Friends (ITV, Rollem & Tiger Aspect, 1999–)
Galaxy Quest (Parisot 1990)
Grey's Anatomy (ABC 2005–)
Heroes (NBC 2006–)
Lost (ABC 2004–)
Misery (Reiner 1990)
My Life with Count Dracula (Black 2003)
One Summer (YTV 1983)
Oprah Winfrey Show (Harpo Productions 1986–)
Perfect Strangers (Stephen Poliakoff 2001)
Playing the Field (Tiger Aspect for BBC 1995)
Quantum Leap (NBC 1989–93)
Red Dwarf (BBC 1988–99)
Sex and the City (HBO, Darren Star, 1998–2004)
Shameless (Channel 4, Paul Abbott, 2004–)
Six Feet Under (HBO, Alan Ball, 2001–5)
The Sopranos (HBO, David Chase, 1999–2007)
Spaced (Paramount 1999–2001)
Star Wars (George Lucas 1977)
State of Play (Paul Abbott, BBC, 2003)
Strictly Come Dancing (BBC1 2004–)
Survivor (CBS 2000–; ITV 2001–)
The Swan (Fox 2004–5)
Ten Years Younger (Channel 4 2004–)
Top Gear (BBC 1978–)
Top Gun (Tony Scott 1986)
Toy Story 2 (John Lasseter 1999)
Trekkies (Nygard 1997)
Twin Peaks (ABC, Frost/Lynch, 1990–1)
Ugly Betty (ABC 2006–)
What Not to Wear (BBC2 2001–4; BBC1 2004–)
Wife Swap (RDF Media, Channel 4, 2003–)
The Wire (HBO, David Simon, 2002–8)
X-Factor (UK) (ITV 2006–)

Index